EVA PENDAELI'S
Original
TANZANIA
COOK
BOOK

EVA PENDAELI–SARAKIKYA

MKUKI NA NYOTA

DAR – ES – SALAAM

PUBLISHED BY
Mkuki na Nyota Publishers Ltd
P.O.Box 4246
Dar es Salaam, Tanzania
www.mkukinanyota.com
publish@mkukinanyota.com

First Published by Tanzania Publishing House, 1978.

Reprinted
1981, 1996, 2013
Redesigned and Reprinted
2019, 2022

ISBN 997 6101 2 52 (10 digits)
ISBN 978 9976 101 25 6 (13 digits)

Visit www.mkukinanyota.com to read more about and to purchase any of Mkuki na Nyota books.
You will also find featured authors interviews and news about other publisher/author events.
Sign up for our e-newsletters for updates on new releases and other announcements.
Distributed worldwide outside Africa by African Books Collective.
www.africanbookscollective.com

Contents

Preface

Tanzanian cookery is a combination of many things: delicious, traditional recipes; new and old methods of food preparation; the wide variety of fruits and vegetables available from fields and markets, staple grains and roots, local spices; fish from the ocean and many rivers and lakes. The recipes I have collected in this *Tanzania Cookbook* strike a balance between good nutrition and good taste, based on foods locally grown and produced. I believe the general public will find this book a treasure as much as secondary school domestic science students. Mothers and rural health workers or anyone interested in the nutrition of babies and young children will find the recipes noted as suitable for young children especially helpful.

This book is not a 'methods' book; for that there are other general books available as well as the wealth of practical experience accumulated among good cooks throughout Tanzania.

New cooks will find that their ability increases through practice and experimentation, such as following my suggestions to substitute one fruit or vegetable for another, depending on the supply available.

Eva Pendaeli Sarakikya
16 August 1977

How to Use This Book

Since the writing of this book the cost of living has more than doubled, oftentimes without a corresponding increase in income. People therefore have tried to adjust their food preparation and consumption. This part of the book should help users to alter recipes according to their needs.

Recipe Selection

This book uses ingredients which may not always be available in some places or which the user may find too expensive. Similarly, some equipment used here may not be available in some homes and institutions. In spite of such difficulties an intelligent cook can select recipes and alter them to meet her immediate needs.

Ingredient substitution or omission

Before deciding on which recipe to use, read carefully the ingredients and method. Note the principal method or methods involved (e.g. stewing, baking, deep frying, etc.) and the equipment required. When omission or substitution of ingredients seems necessary, do not merely look at the ingredients; read again the whole recipe to understand the cooking principles involved and get a clear picture of the finished dish. Then make alterations based on the understanding of these principles. For example, if a doughnut recipe calls for the use of yeast, it would be unwise to omit the yeast because this is the raising agent that provides air for 'raising' the doughnut. Instead, baking powder can be used to perform the same function as yeast. But this means the method for preparation will have to be altered slightly because, while yeast requires time to 'grow' and produce the required air, baking powder does not need such time; to leave it standing in a wet mixture will allow all the air produced to escape. Therefore, while baking powder can be a substitute for yeast in certain recipes, this substitution calls for alterations in the method of preparation and cooking.

On the other hand, if a stew recipe calls for the use of two tomatoes and two onions, the amounts of both these ingredients can be reduced to cut down costs; at the same time, tomato puree or tomato paste can be used instead of fresh tomatoes and vice versa. These changes will alter the richness of the dish, but they will require little or no alterations in the method of preparation. Similarly many of the spices used in the recipes can be reduced in quantity and some can be omitted altogether, provided these are not the key ingredients which either distinguish the dish from any other, or are necessary to give it its peculiar quality. For example, coconut milk can be omitted or substituted for in some chicken stews and sauces, but it is an essential ingredient for 'Coconut Chicken'. What one will have to do if coconut is not available is cook the chicken stew based on the same method and use another ingredient to provide the liquid.

PREPARATION AND SERVING EQUIPMENT

Sometimes it is not possible to get all the equipment and utensils called for by some of the recipes in this book. The reader should study the recipe carefully, as before, to get the underlying principle involved, get a clear picture of the finished product, then decide whether it is possible to substitute equipment or improvise it. For example, for steaming some dishes, an ordinary saucepan can be used instead of steamer; a larger bottle lid or cup can be used instead of a biscuit (pastry) cutter. However, where equipment substitution or improvisation is likely to produce very bad results, then the recipe must not be attempted. For example, a cake recipe that requires a very accurate temperature cannot be made in an improvised oven whose temperature cannot be controlled.

Cooking Times

In this book cooking times, especially for meat and chicken dishes, are approximate. When preparing dishes with these ingredients it is important to determine the cooking time based on the quality of the meat that is being use. The quality (tenderness) of meat varies greatly, and most times this meat is not sold according to the cut (i.e. part of animal from which it is sliced). In addition, the cooking time should be determined based on the intensity of the source of heat used. For example, a burning yellow flame form firewood would be slower than a burning blue flame from a gas cooker.

It is hoped that this brief guideline will assist users of this book.

Guide to Measurements

Approximate equivalents have been used in order to make conversion easier:

1 ounce is taken as 30 grams

1 pint is taken as ½ litre

1 inch is taken as 2 centimetres

Abbreviations	Equivalent Measures
oz = ounce(s)	1 tablespoon flour = 1oz = 30gm
1b = pound(s)	1 tablespoon flour = 1oz = 30gm
gm = gram(s)	1 tablespoon sugar = 1oz = 30gm
kg = kilogramme(s)	2 tablespoon oil = 1oz = 30gm
lt = litre	1 cup flour = 8oz = ¼kg
pt = pint	1 cup liquid = ½pt = ¼little

Guide to Oven Measurements

Oven Heat	Gas Mark	Degrees Fahrenheit	Degrees Centigrade
Very Cool	¼ - ½	200 - 250	100 – 121
Slow	1 – 2	250 – 300	121 – 150
Moderate	3 – 4	325 – 350	160 – 175
Fairly Hot	5 – 4	375 – 400	190 – 205
Fairly Hot	5 – 6	425 – 450	205 - 232
Hot	7 – 8	475	246
Very Hot	8 – 9		

Guide to Spices Commonly Used in Tanzania

GINGER (*Tangawizi*) A root spice available whole or ground. Used in curries, tea, and other beverages. Also cakes, sweets, puddings, pickles, and other preserves, and also as medicine.

TURMERIC (*Manjano*) A root spice, bright yellow in colour. Used in flavouring savoury dishes, in relishes and pickles, and as an ingredient in curry powder. For colouring other spices and dyeing.

GARLIC (*Kitunguu Sumu* or *Kitunguu Saumu*) A bulb of the onion family. It is made up of small parts stuck together in a bundle. These parts are referred to as 'cloves' of garlic. It has very strong flavour and is used in small quantities in curries, relishes and other strongly flavoured savoury dishes.

CINNAMON (*Mdalasini*) A spice from the bark of a tree. It has a delicate flavour and the curled strips of the bark are known as cinnamon sticks, used whole for flavouring savoury dishes- pilau, pickles, etc. Ground cinnamon is also used for flavouring both savoury and sweet dishes, beverages and cooked fruits.

ix

PEPPERS (*Pilipili Manga*) Both the ground black and white pepper are dried, unripe berries of a creeping plant. The difference between the two peppers lies in their preparation. The peppers are also available whole, and when ground at home give the best flavour. Pepper is mostly used as a condiment at the table in savoury dishes and sauces.

SWEET PEPPER (*Pilipili Hoho*) Sometimes known as Italian pepper. It has mild flavour except for the seeds which have a strong flavour. When fresh it is used as a vegetable, and sometimes to flavour other vegetable dishes, rice sauces and fish. The ripe peppers which are red or yellow in colour are usually pickled or canned.

CHILLI PEPPER (*Pilipili Kali*) A pod of a plant of the same family as cayenne paprika and sweet peppers. Chilli pepper is very hot to taste and is mostly used for flavouring savoury dishes requiring a hot taste and in pickles and chutneys. When fresh it is green and when ripe it is bright red. The ripe pepper is dried and ground, also used in making curry powder.

CORIANDER (*Giligiliani*) These are seeds of a *kotimiri* plant, with a mild, distinctive flavour. Used whole in savoury dishes, e.g. pilau, in relishes and pickles and ground in sweet, biscuits, in the making of curry powder. The leaves are known as *kotimiri* and sold fresh in making masala for rich savoury dishes, e.g. *kuku paka*, *samaki rojo* and curries.

CARDAMON (*Iliki*) These are seeds of a reed-like plant, also grown in Tanzania; the seeds are contained in a capsule. It has a pleasantly strong flavour and is used in beverages, pickles, rice dishes and curry powders.

CUMIN (*Bizari Nyembamba*) These are thin seeds of a plant, an ancient favourite of the Mediterranean. In this country it is used in rice, pilau, in sweets prepared by Asians, bread, stews and meat dishes for those who like the pungent aroma it gives.

MUSTARD (*Haradali*) These are seeds of a plant, the two varieties are back mustard seeds and white mustard seeds. The seeds are used whole in fried foods, e.g. *chapati*, in meat, and pickles. Ground mustard is normally used as a condiment.

CLOVES (*Karafuu*) These are dried, unopened flower buds, grown mainly in Zanzibar. Used for making oil mixed with other oil for cooking, as a spice in stews, rice dishes, pilau, fruit puddings, sweets and cakes. Also used for manufacture of perfumes.

NUTMEG and MACE (*Kungu*) The two spices are produced from the fruit of the same tree. The mace is the outer covering of the fruit and the nutmeg is the seed or kernel of this fruit. Mace is used in savoury dishes and pickles, nutmeg is used mainly in sweet dishes, cakes, beverages and occasionally vegetables.

ALLSPICE This spice is dried seeds of a tree. Its aroma and taste seem to be a combination of cinnamon, cloves and nutmeg. When ground, allspice is used in many spice blends, e.g. mixed spices and as a flavouring in meat and vegetable dishes, sweets, puddings, cakes and soups. Whole allspice is used for preserve and chutneys.

CURRY POWDER This is a very popular mixture of different spices. It normally includes ground curry, turmeric, ginger, cardamom, cinnamon, chillies and sometimes a few other spices. Curry powder varies in the amount of each spice used; this variation determines the quantity, aroma and cost of the finished product.

I. Beverages

Tea

4 cups water

2 level teaspoons tea leaves

4 teaspoons sugar to taste milk

1. Put the water to boil. 2. When hot pour some about one cup into the teapot or jug in which the tea is to be served in order to warm it up. 3. When the water boils, pour out the water from the teapot, add tea leaves then pour the boiling water over it. 4. Leave to stand for a few minutes to steep. 5. Serve hot on a tray with hot or cold milk and sugar.

Coffee

4 cups water

1 cup milk, if desired

1 tablespoon ground coffee

sugar to taste

1. Put the water to boil. 2. When hot, pour some about one cup, into the jug or coffee pot in which the coffee is to be served in order to warm it up. 3. To the remaining water add the ground coffee. Cover. 4. Lower the heat and simmer very gently for 5-7 minutes. 5. Empty

the water from the jug or coffee pot. 6. Strain the coffee into the warm jug or pot. 7. Serve with hot milk and sugar.

COCOA

1 or 2 cups milk

1 cup water

2 level teaspoons cocoa

sugar to taste

1. Make a thin paste of cocoa and a little milk in a cup. 2. Put the remaining milk, or milk and water, in a pan to boil. 3. When the milk starts to boil, add the cocoa mixture. Rinse the cup into the milk. Stir well. 4. Boil for 5 minutes. 5. Pour the cocoa into a warm pot and serve hot.

NOTE: The cocoa pot can be warmed by rinsing with hot water.

PAWPAW JUICE

small, ripe pawpaw, whole or sliced

sugar (optional)

Cold water

lime

1.Choose a soft, ripe pawpaw. 2. Peel, mash and press through a fine sieve. 3. Add sugar (if used) fresh lime juice and enough cold water to make required consistency. 4. Stir well and serve cold.

PASSION FRUIT JUICE (ZABIBU)

4-6 ripe passion fruit

sugar to taste

soda water or plain cold water according to taste

1.Wash and break passion fruit into a bowl. 2. Stir thoroughly without breaking seeds. 3. Strain into a jug. Add sugar, water or soda to taste and stir. 4. Serve cold.

APPLE JUICE

2 fresh medium apples

1 tablespoon lemon/lime juice

2 cherries for decoration (Optional)

2 tablespoons sugar

1 pt (½ Lt) water

food colouring

1.Wash and peel apples. Cut them open and remove the core. Sprinkle with lemon juice to avoid discoloration. 2. Slice apples and put them in a pan. Add sugar and water and cook till soft. 3. Mash. 4. Strain out juice into clean glasses. 5. Add colouring. 6. Decorate with cherries and put in a cool place or refrigerator. 7. Serve cold.

PINEAPPLE MILK SHAKE

1 glass boiled, cold milk

½ glass pineapple juice or large, very ripe pineapple

2 teaspoons sugar

few ice cubes (optional)

1. Make pineapple juice as follows: a) Slice and mash up pineapple thoroughly. b) Squeeze out juice using a fine sieve or clean muslin. 2. Put milk, juice and sugar into a crew top jar or bottle, or a shaker, and shake vigorously. 3. Serve at once.

NOTE: a) Where a refrigerator is available, both milk and juice should be ice cold before shaking or a few ice cubes should be used when shaking. b) Other fruits such as lemon, apricot, bananas, oranges, peaches and pawpaw can be used to make fruit drinks of different flavours. The juice or pulp of each fruit is prepared according to the kind of fruit.

PINEAPPLE EGG NOG

1 egg

½ glass cold, boiled milk

A few ice cubes (if available)

2 teaspoons sugar

¼ glass pineapple juice

1. Separate egg white from the yolk. 2. Whisk egg yolk and sugar until creamy. 3. Pour milk, whisked egg mixture, pineapple juice and ice, if used, into a shaker or screw-top jar and shake vigorously. 4. Whisk egg white until stiff, then fold into egg mixture and serve immediately.

LEMON SQUASH

1 lemon

2-3 glasses water

1 tablespoon sugar

1. Wash lemon and cut off rind. 2. Boil rind in water for a few minutes to extract flavour. 3. Cut and squeeze out lemon and strain juice into a jug or mug. 4. Add sugar and water in which rind was boiled. Add more cold water if desired. 5. Cover and put to cool in a refrigerator or cold place before serving. It should serve 1-2 glasses.

NOTE: a) A quicker method is to squeeze the juice and strain it in enough cold water. Add desired amount of sugar. Shake well and serve. b) Other fruits such as oranges, lime, grapefruits can be made into squashes. They can be prepared in the same way as the lemon squash.

LIME DRINK

3-4 ripe limes

2 glasses cold water or

1 glass water

1 glass soda water

2 tablespoons sugar

1. Wash limes, cut and squeeze out juice into a jug or mug. 2. Add water and sugar, pour into a bottle. 3. Shake thoroughly. 4. Serve cold.

GRAPE FRUIT DRINK

1 ripe grapefruit

2 tablespoons sugar

2–3 glasses water

Prepare as for lime drink.

5

2
SOUPS AND SAUCES

MIXED VEGETABLE SOUP

1 small onion, finely chopped

salt and pepper to taste

1 oz (30 gm) cabbage, finely Shredded

meat or chicken stock 1 pt water

1 small carrot, finely shredded

1 teaspoon oil or fat

½ potato, finely shredded

1 clove garlic

1 small stalk diced celery

½ teaspoon parsley, chopped

1. Wash all vegetables before cutting. 2. Heat the fat and fry the onion and garlic lightly. Add the vegetables and seasoning and sautee for a few minutes before adding liquid. 3. Add water or stock and cook gently until the vegetables are tender, about 30 – 40 minutes. Taste for seasoning. 4. Serve hot.

DRY BEAN SOUP

4 oz (120 gm) beans

2 tomatoes

1 onion

salt to taste

1 tablespoon cooking fat

1 teaspoon curry powder

½ teaspoon chilli powder

½ pt (¼ Litre) coconut milk

1. Soak beans overnight. 2. Remove skins and wash beans. 3. Boil the beans until cooked. 4. Drain the water and mash them finely. 5. Chop the onion and the tomatoes. 6. Fry onion until brown. 7. Add in tomatoes, curry powder and chilli powder. 8. Add in mashed beans and fry together for 7 minutes. 9. Add in coconut milk and more water if necessary. 10. Simmer for 15 minutes. 11. Serve hot.

CREAMED PEA SOUP

16 oz (500 gm) shelled peas

1 large onion, chopped

1 pt (½Litre) water for boiling or stock

salt and pepper to taste

1/8pt (1/16 Litre) cream (optional)

1 teaspoon butter ,(if cream is not used)

1. Wash peas. Put to boil using water or stock. Add onion, herbs and seasoning. 2. When cooked and soft, test for seasoning, mash. Dilute with hot water or stock if necessary. 3. Put through a sieve. Re-heat, remove from heat and add cream.

NOTE: Once cream is added the soup must not be boiled, as it will curdle; if cream is not used, add one-teaspoon butter.

PUMPKIN CREAMED SOUP

1½ lb (¾ kg) meat bones or meat with bone

1 small onion

salt to taste

12 oz (360gm) pumpkin

1½ pt (¾ Litre) water

1/8pt (1/16 Litre) cream

1. Peel and split onion into halves. 2. Wash, peel and cut pumpkin into even sixes, removing seeds and pith. 3. Wash again to remove excessive sap. 4. Put onion, salt and bones to boil for 45-60 minutes. Add the pumpkins and cook until the pumpkin is thoroughly cooked. 5. Remove bones and onion and whisk the soup thoroughly. Dilute with hot water if necessary. 6. Re-heat, remove from heat, then add cream. 7. Serve hot.

NOTE: Do not boil the soup once the cream is added.

PUMPKIN SOUP (PUMPKIN MTORI)

16 oz (500 gm) meat with bones

1 small onion.

1 teaspoon salt

12 oz (360 gm) pumpkin

¼ pt (1/8 Litre) coconut milk (optional)

½ oz (15 gm) butter

1 clove garlic

1½ pt (¾ Litre) water

1. Peel and split onion and garlic into two halves. 2. Peel and cut pumpkin, meat, salt and water in a deep pan, bring to boil, then reduce heat and simmer for 1-1½ hours,

or until meat is tender. Add coconut milk and simmer for another 15-20 minutes. 4. Remove bones and onions.

Whisk soup thoroughly. Dilute with hot water if necessary. Add butter, re-heat and serve hot separately with meat.

NOTE: If tough meat such as shin beef or oxtail is used it will need cooking until almost done before adding pumpkins.

BANANA SOUP (NDIZI MTORI)

This is a traditional dish for nursing mothers and children around Kilimanjaro area.

3 (½ kg) soft green bananas

1-1½ lb (¾ kg) meat, with bones

1 large potato

1 clove garlic, chopped

1 medium onion, chopped

½ oz butter

salt to taste

1½ pt (¾ Litre) water

1. Peel, slice bananas lengthwise, removing the seeded pith (centre). Wash in hot water. 2. Wash meat and leave whole, but if the bone is too big or long, cut the meat up. 3. Put all ingredients except butter in a deep pan, add water, bring to the boil, reduce heat and simmer for 1-1½ hours. 4. Remove meat, whisk the soup thoroughly. Add butter, re-heat and serve hot.

NOTE: ¼ pt coconut milk can be added about 10 – 15 minutes before whisking.

CHICKEN AND CASSAVA SOUP (CASSAVA MTORI)

1½ lb (¾ kg) chicken bones or
carcass or well-cleaned chicken legs

1 lb (½ kg) fresh cassava

1 medium onion

2 cloves garlic

1 cup coconut milk (Optional)

Optional

1 green chilli

pinch of ground cloves (optional)

salt to taste

water

1 dessertspoon tomato

puree or 1 fresh tomato

2 oz (60 gm) ghee

1. Peel cassava, cut into half, lengthwise and remove the pith. 2. Cut into fairly small pieces and wash in boiling water. 3. Wash and boil chicken bones or carcass for a while about 30 minutes. 4. Peel and chop onion and garlic, green chilli. 5. Add into the boiling chicken, the onion, garlic, chilli, ghee and cassava. 6. Add in salt, ground cloves and tomato and leave to simmer until the cassava is thoroughly cooked. 7. Add coconut milk. 8. Bring to boil and leave to simmer for another 10–15 minutes. 9. Remove chicken. 10. Mash the mixture thoroughly, whisk and dilute with hot water or thin coconut milk if necessary. 11. Re-heat and serve hot.

NOTE: If the soup looks stringy, pass it through a sieve before heating. The thread-like roots result from poor quality cassava.

TRIPE SOUP (TRIPE MTORI)

1 lb (½ kg) tripe

6 large green bananas, soft type (*matoke*)

1 large tomato, sliced

1 larger onion, sliced

½ oz (15 gm) or

1 level tablespoon ghee

3 clove garlic, chopped

1 lime or lemon

1 coconut

salt and pepper to taste

1. Wash meat several times in cold, salty water. 2. Boil sweet bread in a strong stewing pan. Add in lime juice. 3. Peel bananas and remove the inside hard core. Cut bananas into thin strips and wash well in cold water or boil to remove sticky sap if bananas are very young. 5. Add bananas, onion, tomato and seasonings into the boiling meat and cook until meat and bananas are soft, (about 1½ hours). 6. Add in more water if necessary. 7. Make about ½ pt strong coconut milk. Add to the pan. 8. Cook for another 10 -15 minutes. 9. Remove meat, put onto a clean plate and cut into pieces. 10. Mash bananas until soft using a potato masher or a wooden spoon, then whisk thoroughly. Add cut-up meat. 11. Re-heat and serve hot.

TOMATO AND ONION SAUCE

1 large onion

2 large tomatoes

1 teaspoon turmeric

2 tablespoons oil or 1 oz (30gm) fat

1 tablespoon lemon juice

⅛ Litre coconut milk or stock salt and pepper to taste ¼ pt

1. Peel and chop onion, tomatoes and garlic. 2. Put all ingredients except liquid in a pan and slowly cook covered until onion and tomatoes are very soft. Stir well. 3. Add either coconut milk or stock. Stir well and continue to cook for 10–15 minutes. When ready, the sauce should be of coating consistency. 4. Use as required.

NOTE: Cooked vegetables can be added to this sauce; sometimes the liquid is omitted if a drier mixture is desired.

GROUNDNUT SAUCE - method I

4 oz (120 gm) roasted groundnuts

1 tomato

1 onion

½ oz (15 gm) fat

1 teaspoon curry powder

½ pt (¼ Litre)water

juice of ½ lemon

1. Peel and chop onions and tomatoes into very fine pieces. 2. Melt fat, gently fry onions, add tomatoes, curry powder, pepper salt and lemon juice. 3. Grind groundnuts and sieve them to obtain course flour. Put flour in ¼ litre water, stir until well-mixed. 4. Pour the mixture over frying onions and tomatoes. 5. Lower heat, stirring constantly; simmer gently until groundnuts are cooked. 6. Serve hot with rice plus a vegetable, e.g. fried cabbage.

COCONUT SAUCE

12 oz (360 gm) tomatoes (about 2 large)

4 oz (120 gm) onions (about 2)

4-3 cloves garlic

2 teaspoons turmeric

2 teaspoons salt

1 pt (½ Litre) coconut milk, made from 1 coconut chilli powder or fresh chilli to taste

fresh chilli to taste

1 tablespoon fat or

2 tablespoons oil

1½ bunch *kotimiri* (mixed herbs)

1. Wash, peel and slice tomatoes and *kotimiri*. 2. Peel and chop onions and garlic. 3. Put vegetables, seasoning and fat in a pan and slowly cook covered until onions and

tomatoes are very soft. Stir well and add coconut milk. Continue cooking, stirring constantly for another 10–15 minutes or until mixture thickens, and the coconut is cooked. 5. Use as required.

MAMUMUNYA (GOURD) SAUCE

1½ lb (¾ kg) *mamumunya*

1 large onion

1 large tomato

¾ cloves garlic

½ bundle *kotimiri*

½ pt (¼lt) coconut milk

1 teaspoonful turmeric

1 tablespoon fat

1 lime or lemon

salt to taste

1. Peel and slice onions, tomatoes and garlic. 2. Wash *kotimiri* and chop. 3. Wash thinly, peel and evenly slice the gourds, removing excessive seeds and core. Put in salty water. 4. Fry onion lightly, add tomatoes, seasonings and herbs. Cover, lower heat and cook for 5-10 minutes. Add gourds and continue to cook with ¼ of the coconut milk and simmer for 5-10 minutes. 5. Add the remaining cocnut milk and simmer for 5-10 minutes. 6. Serve hot as a vegetable.

NOTE: To taste for a young gourd, a delicate nail should easily pierce the skin. Medium sixes are better, as the larger ones are normally older and therefore hard and seedy.

BRINGAL SAUCE

8 oz (240 gm) *bringals*

1 large onion

3 tablespoons oil

1 green chilli

½ lemon

2-3 cloves garlic

1-2 large tomatoes or 2 tablespoons tomato paste

salt to taste

1 teaspoon turmeric

1/8 water, if tomato paste is used

1. Wash, peel and slice onion and tomatoes. 2. Heat the fat in a pan, fry onion slightly. Add chilli, turmeric, lemon juice and salt. 3. Add peeled and sliced *bringals*, fry for a few minutes. 4. Add tomatoes. Lower heat and simmer covered until vegetables are tender. If tomato paste is used, add hot water, then simmer.

NOTE: The *bringals* should be peeled and sliced just before they are required, otherwise they turn dirty brown. Excess seeds should cut as these have a strong flavour.

GROUNDNUT SAUCE - method 2

4 oz (120 gm) roasted groundnuts

1 medium tomato, chopped

1 medium onion, chopped

¾ pt (⅜ Litre) coconut milk a little water to mix

1. Prepare groundnut flour: skin groundnuts. Grind groundnuts until very fine; use a sieve to get even finer flour. 2. Mix groundnut flour with a little water to make a smooth paste. 3. Cook coconut milk, tomatoes and onions until soft. 4. Pour in groundnut paste until it boils, stirring with a wooden spoon to avoid lumps. 5. Simmer covered for half an hour. Serve as a sauce for a main dish, such as rice, *ugali* and some vegetables.

COCONUT MILK - method 1

1 medium coconut

1 pt (¼ Litre) warm water.

1. Break coconut in two halves. 2. Grate coconut by using a coconut grater (*mbuzi*) or remove the nut from the shell and grate it over a hand grater. 3. Put grated coconut in a larger bowl. 4. Mix half pint of warm water in with the grated coconut. Squeeze the coconut to extract juice and fat. 5. Pour the whole mixture through a sieve into another bowl. Squeeze out the liquid from the grated coconut remaining on the sieve to obtain the remaining juice and fat. 6. Repeat the same procedure with the other half pint of water.

NOTE: The amount of liquid and its thickness vary according to the taste or the needs of a given recipe.

COCONUT MILK - method 2

coconut as required

water (hot), as required

1. Grate the required amount of coconut. 2. Measure out required amount of hot water. Put grated coconut in a container and add hot water. 3. Wash your hands and use them to squeeze the grated coconut in the water. 4. Use a sieve to strain the milk. Squeeze the coconut until dry. 5. Use the coconut as required.

NOTE: Instead of a sieve, a muslin cloth may be used. After getting the first "*tui*", more hot water (as required) can be added to the coconut to produce a second "*tui*" which is not as strong as the first.

AVOCADO SALAD CREAM

1 ripe avocado

½ lemon juice 1½ tablespoon salad cream

1. Wash avocado peel and cut it into four slices. 2. Remove the seed and inner skin. 3. Peel off the outer cover and cut into very small pieces into a bowl. 4. Mash them and pass the mixture through a sieve. 5. Add salad cream and lemon juice and bet well. 6. Pour into a sauceboat an serve with cooked or raw vegetable salad.

3
VEGETABLES

CURRIED MIXED VEGETABLES

16 oz (½ kg) shelled peas

8 oz (¼ kg) *bringals*

16 oz (½ kg) carrots and potatoes

2 large tomatoes

Masala

3-4 cloves garlic, crushed

1 teaspoon turmeric

1 teaspoon salt

1 teaspoon curry powder

1-2 green chilles, finely chopped or ¼ teaspoon chilli powder

1 teaspoon curry powder or

1 Lime

1. Peel and dice carrots, potatoes and *bringals*. 2. Steam or boil carrots peas and potatoes, starting with carrots. 3. Mix one tablespoon oil with lime juice, garlic and the rest of the seasonings. 4. Heat remaining fat. Add chopped tomatoes, masala and diced *bringals*. Cook covered until tender. Add the other cooked vegetables and continue cooking for a few more minutes. There should be no need to add water. Serve hot.

NOTE: If possible, it is better to steam the peas, carrots and potatoes, to preserve the nutritive value and also avoid the necessity of disposing of surplus water from the boiled vegetables.

MIXED VEGETABLE FLAN

Cheese pastry

4 oz (120 gm) plain flour
1 oz (30 gm) grated cheese
1 oz (30 gm) fat
pinch of salt and pepper
1 oz (30 gm) margarine
cold water and lemon juice for mixing

Filling

2 eggs
3 medium tomatoes
1 oz (30 gm) grated cheese
¼ pt (1/8lt) fresh milk
1 small carrot
parsley
2 oz (60 gm) shelled peas

Oven temperature

R 6 (40ºF - 20ºC)

1. Pre-heat oven. 2. Prepare pastry. Sift flour, salt and pepper into a bowl. Rub in the fat, margarine and cheese. Add enough cold water mixed with the lemon juice to make a firm dough. Mix well with the fingers but do not knead. Roll out the pastry and line a 7" flan tin or roll out to the shape of the baking dish. Press the pastry well into the sides. Trim round the edges and prick the bottom. Bake blind for 20 minutes. 3. Prepare filling. Wash, scrape and thinly slice the carrot. Cook peas and carrots in boiling salted water. Peel and slice potatoes into strips. Add them to the cooking carrot after 10 minutes or so. Skin and cut up two of the tomatoes. Beat eggs and mix with cheese, tomato, milk and seasonings. Mix well with boiled vegetables. Do not include the stock. 4. Pour the mixture into the flan case. Sprinkle with cheese and put into the hot oven for 15-20 minutes. Reduce heat after 15 minutes. 5. Garnish the flan with grilled tomatoes and parsley. 6. Serve at once.

18 VEGETABLE PANCAKE ROLLS

Batter

4 oz (120 gm) plain four

1 egg

pinch salt

½ pt (¼lt) water

Filling

4 oz (120 gm) shelled peas or *mbaazi*

1 teaspoon chopped *kotimiri,*

4 oz (120 gm) chopped spinach

½ tablespoon ghee

1 medium carrot

salt to taste

1 medium onion

fat for deep-fat frying

1. Make batter. Sift flour and salt into a bowl. Make a well in the centre. Break egg, beat it up and mix it with the water. Pour the mixture in the well and gradually stir in the flour to a pouring consistency. Cover with a clean towel and keep in a cool place.

Prepare filling: Wash and scrape the carrot. Dice it up into small pieces. Shell and wash peas and cook them in boiling salted water until half-cooked. Add carrot in to cook with the peas. Wash and very finely chop the spinach. Chop onion, green pepper and *kotimiri* and mix them well. Fry the onion. Add spinach, salt and all other spices (ground ginger, *kotimiri*, pepper). Add cooked peas and carrot and mix well. Taste for seasoning, preseason if necessary, cook till fairly dry. Leave them until cold. 3. Oil a heavy-based frying pan, very lightly and heat slightly. Pour batter on the hot frying pan and move it from side to tide until the bottom is completely covered. Raise the heat and cook pancake on one side only. Remove from the pan.

To prepare pancake rolls: 5. Put a teaspoon of the filling on one half of the pancake and roll over lengthwise. Seal the edges with flour paste. 6. Heat oil in a deep frying pan and deep fat-fry them until golden brown. 7. Drain them on an absorbent paper. 8. Serve with wedges of lemon.

NOTE: These are good for snacks, parties, etc. The filling can be made from left-over food.

STIR-FRY VEGETABLES

4–6 oz (120–180 gm) fillet or lean beef or 4 oz (120 gm) fish steak

2-3 eggs

Choose at least two or three of these vegetables:

3 oz (90 gm) lettuce, shredded

6 oz (120 gm) cucumber, dice

6 oz (180 gm) carrots, or coarse grated

6 oz (180 gm) tomatoes, chopped

6 oz (120 gm) cabbage, shredded

3 oz (90 gm) green pepper, chopped

2 oz (60 gm) spinach, coarse chopped

1 cup water or stock

2 teaspoons corn flour

2-3 tablespoons oil

2 tablespoon soy sauce

1. Cut all vegetables as indicated. 2. Cut meat, fish or poultry into small pieces, preferably thin strips or cubes. If eggs are used, scramble or boil and chop. Pre-cook meat, boil or fry. 3. Heat cooking oil in a deep frying pan or saucepan. 4. Fry hardest vegetables first, e.g. carrots, then add the rest so that the softest is put in last. 5. Continue to fry for a while then add the water or stock and simmer for a few minutes. 6. Mix corn flour with a little water into a smooth paste. Add soy sauce. 7. Add sauce and meat, if used, to the cooking vegetables. Continue to cook until the starch cooks and thickness the sauce and vegetables are cooked but still crisp. 8. Taste for salt and serve immediately with rice.

NOTE: More soy sauce can be added if desired.

FRIED GOURDS (MAMUMUNYA)

2 medium young gourds

½ teaspoon curry powder

1 large fresh tomato or 1 tablespoon tomato paste

1½ tablespoon ghee or fat

salt

1 onion

1 egg

1. Peel gourds and cut them into fairly small pieces, removing excess seeds. 2. Wash and steam or cook them in a little boiling water until just done. 3. Boil egg for about 10 minutes. Peel and chop. 4. Skin and cut up tomato. 5. Peel and chop onion very finely. 6. Heat oil in a frying pan and fry onions. 7. Add tomatoes, curry powder and salt. Lower heat. Cook covered until soft. 8. Add gourds and cook while covered for 5 minutes more. 9. Serving: Put the fried gourds in serving dish and sprinkle chopped egg over it. 10. This can be served as a vegetable with starchy foods, e.g. rice.

MAIZE AND SPINACH MIX (NTUNYULA)

8 oz (240 gm) spinach (*mchicha*)

2 tablespoons cooking oil or fat.

6 oz (180 gm) green maize, off the cob

salt to taste

1. Wash maize well until all silky threads are removed. 2. Cook in a little boiling salted water. 3. Wash and cut spinach very finely. 4. When maize kernels are nearly cooked, add spinach and cook until the kernels and spinach are tender and the water considerable reduced. 5. Add cooking oil. Mix well and leave to cook for 5-10 minutes. 6. Cool and serve cold with sour milk or yogurt.

NOTE: Alternatively, maize can be steamed.

CAULIFLOWER PILAU

small cauliflower

½ teaspoon curry powder

1 cup rice

1 small onion

1 carrot

¾ cup roasted, skinned groundnuts, finely chopped

2 cardamom pods

2 cloves

1 tablespoon fat

salt to taste

1. Chop up cauliflower and wash several times in salty water. 2. Wash and soak rice. 3. Skin and chop onion. 4. Scrape and thinly slice carrot. 5. Heat fat in a pan and fry onion but do not brown. Add sliced carrot and seasoning i.e. curry powder, cloves, cardamom and salt. 6. Add the rice and fry for a while and then add the chopped cauliflower. 7. Add about 2 cups water to groundnuts and mix well. 8. Add this to rice and cauliflower, stir. 9. Lower heat and cook gently, stirring occasionally until rice is soft. 10. Add a knob of fat on top and put pan in a moderately hot oven from 10-10 minutes or put hot charcoal on a metal lid and place on top of the pan. 11. Garnish with tomato and parsley and serve hot for lunch or dinner.

 ## TWO -VEGETABLE SAUCE

½ lb (¼ kg) carrots

salt to taste

1 lb (½ kg) shelled peas

½ teaspoon carry powder

1 small onion

¼ teaspoon turmeric (optional)

1 large tomato or

a pinch of chill powder

1 tablespoon

½ pt (1 cup) coconut milk

1 teaspoon Tomato paste

½ lemon or lime

1 desert spoon ghee

1. Prepare coconut milk. 2. Skin and chop onion very finely. 3. Skin and slice tomato (if fresh). Wash, scrape and dice carrots. Wash peas. 4. Collect all dry ingredients and make a paste with a little lemon juice. 5. Heat fat in a saucepan and fry onion lightly. Add tomato, all seasoning and carrots and fry for a while. 7. Add peas, then coconut milk and stir until it thickens. 8. Cover and leave to cook till carrots and peas are soft and cooked. 9. Serve hot with *ugali* or rice.

NOTE: Good for vegetarian diets.

GROUNDNUT VEGETABLE STEW

2 medium onions

1 teaspoon vegetable extract, if available

1 small red pepper

2 medium tomatoes

3 oz (90 gm) groundnuts

4 small carrots

2 oz (60 gm) fresh or beans

2 tablespoons oil

1 pepper and salt to taste teaspoon chilli powder

1. Roast, shell and grind the groundnuts. Chop onions and pepper. Skin tomatoes and cut into quarters. Peel and slice carrots. 2. Fry onions and pepper in oil. 3. Stir in tomato, carrots, add some liquid. Simmer until soft. Add groundnuts. 4. Add peas or beans, cook an additional 10 minutes. 5. Season with chill, pepper, salt and extract. 6. Serve with rice.

NOTE: If beans are used, soak overnight and boil until tender. To improve nutritional value add some evaporated milk at stage 4.

FRIED BRINGALS

4 small, young *bringals*

2-3 tablespoon ghee or oil for frying

 salt and pepper to taste

2 onions

For coating:

1 egg

dried bread crumbs

1. Wash *bringals* and slice thinly. 2. Place slices in water to which salt and lemon juice have been added. 3. Beat egg, season and pour on a plate. 4. Spread bread crumbs on another plate. 5. Dry *bringal* slices with tea towel, coat with egg then bread crumbs. 6. Fry them in shallow fat. Serve hot as an accompanying vegetable.

NOTE: If *bringals* are more matured, they will have stronger flavour. More seeds which will need reducing bore cooking.

BRINGALS IN COCONUT SAUCE

16 oz (500 gm) *bringals*

salt to taste

1 large onion, chopped

1 tablespoon oil or 1 oz (30 gm) fat

1 teaspoon turmeric

1 clove garlic, chopped

½ pt (¼ litre) coconut *milk*

1 chilli

1 lemon

½ lime

1. Wash *bringals*, peel and slice. Remove excessive seeds if any. Put in water in which salt and lemon juice has been added. 2. Heat fat, add onion, garlic, chilli, salt, turmeric, lime juice and finally dried *bringals*. Fry for a few minutes, stirring carefully so as not to mash *bringals*. 3. Add coconut milk, reduce heat. Cook gently until *bringals* and onion are tender and coconut milk thickens. Taste for salt. 4. Serve hot as a vegetable.

CURRIED BRINGALS

2 lbs (1 kg) young *bringals* (about 4-6)

2-3 cloves garlic

1 teaspoon curry powder

2 large onions, sliced

1 teaspoon turmeric

2 large tomatoes, peeled and chopped

1 chilli powder to taste

¼ pt (1/8lt) water or stock

2 teaspoons tomato paste

2 oz (60 gm) fat

1 lemon

1. Wash *bringals*, peel and slice into fairly thin slices or cubes, removing excessive seeds. 2. Put in water in which salt and lemon juice has been added. This reduces discolouration of *bringals*. 3. Peel and slice potatoes. Put in water. 4. Peel and chop onions, tomatoes and garlic. 5. Collect all dry ingredients in a small basin. Mix with a little oil and lemon juice (equal quantities) to make a paste. Add tomato puree and mix well. 6. Heat the remaining fat, add onions, garlic and fry until golden brown. 7. Drain and dry *bringals* and potatoes. Add onion and fry for about 3 minutes. 8. Add the spice mixture in the basin, then the tomatoes. Cook covered for 5-10 minutes at reduced heat. Add water. 9. Simmer gently until tender and the curry is thick. 10. Serve hot with pilau or chapattis.

STUFFED BRINGALS

4 medium or 2 large *bringals*

½ teaspoon curry powder

1 onion

¼ teaspoon turmeric a pinch of hot chilli, if desired

2 cloves garlic

salt to taste

1 tablespoon tomato paste

1 tablespoon cooking fat

1 lime or lemon

1. Wash *bringals* and cut into half vertically. Partially scoop both halves. Discard excessive seeded parts. Finely slice the remaining scooped part. 2. Peel and chop onions and garlic. 3. Heat the fat, sautee the sliced bringals, onions and garlic until fairly tender. Drain well. 4. Mix chilli, curry powder, turmeric, salt, tomato paste with a

little fat and lime juice in small bowl. Add this mixture to the sautéed vegetables. Mix well. 5. Stuff the scooped *bringals* halves with the above mixture. 6. Put some fat in a large frying pan or saucepan and heat well. 7. Carefully place the stuffed *bringals* over the hot fat. Fry over low heat until tender. If they tend to dry, cover with a lid to keep them moist. 8. Serve with chipped potatoes or cassava.

PEAS PILAU (MCHANYATO)

8 oz (240 gm) rice

½ green chilli

8 oz (240 gm) peas, dried

½ teaspoon cinnamon

1 onion

3 cardamoms

1 medium tomato

2 cloves garlic

1 teaspoon tomato paste

2 oz (6 gm) fat

1 teaspoon curry powder

½ pt (¼ litre) coconut milk

1 teaspoon cumin seeds

1. Parboil peas. 2. Wash and soak rice. 3. Peel and chop tomato, onion and garlic. 4. Fry onion and garlic. Add all spices, lastly tomatoes, and tomato paste. 5. Fry spices, then add peas. 6. Fry for a few minutes and add coconut milk. Add rice, lower heat and simmer until rice and peas are cooked. 7. Serve hot as a main dish.

FRENCH BEANS WITH WHITE SAUCE

8 oz (240 gm) French beans

½ pt (¼lt) milk

1 level teaspoon salt

salt and pepper for sauce

1 oz (30 gm) margarine

1. Prepare French beans by washing and slicing them diagonally. 2. Put them to boil.
3. Prepare white sauce. Melt margarine. Add flour and cook. Add milk a little at a
time while stirring thoroughly. Add salt and pepper. Bring the sauce to boil.
4. When beans are ready, strain off excess liquid. Mix them with sauce. 5. Serve hot as
a vegetable.

VEGETABLE SAMBUSAS

Pastry

4 oz (120 gm) flour

water to make stiff dough

2 tablespoons oil

a pinch of salt

Filling

2 potatoes, shredded

1 teaspoon lemon juice

3 carrots, diced

½ green chilli, chopped

4 tablespoons peas, boiled

2 large onions, finely chopped

1 teaspoon turmeric

1 teaspoon fat

1 level teaspoon salt

1. Heat fat in a pan. Add onions first then the other ingredients, sauté for a while. 2. Cover pan and cook gently until almost done. 3. Remove lid, cook quickly to remove excessive moisture. 4. Leave to cool and use this filling instead of meat. 5. Prepare pastry and the pastry cases as for meat sambusas (see Section 4 Meat, Fish and Poultry). 6. Fry the vegetable sambusas in same manner as meat sambusas.

POTATO BAJIA

4 oz (120 gm) gram flour (*dengu* flour)

¼ pt (⅛ litre) water

4 oz (120 gm) potatoes, peeled

6 cloves garlic, crushed

½ level teaspoon salt

1 green chilli, crushed

oil for deep frying.

1. Sliced potatoes into thin slices. 2. Mix salt, gram flour, crushed garlic and chilli. 3. Add water and mix into a coating consistency. Add potatoes. 4. Using a tablespoon drop mixture to hot fat and fry. 5. Serve hot or cold as a snack.

SAVOURY PUMPKIN PIE

Pastry

4 oz (120 gm) flour

1 tablespoon cooking oil

¼ teaspoon salt

3-4 tablespoon cold water

Filling

1 lb (½ kg) pumpkin, peeled and cut

1 medium onion

2 cloves garlic

1 medium-sized carrot

8 oz (¼ kg) minced meat

Oven temperature

R 6 (40° F – 20°C)

1 Pre-cook minced meat in a little salt. 2. Prepare vegetables. Coarsely shred pumpkin. Scrape carrot and coarsely. Skin and chop onion and garlic cloves. 3. Heat ghee in a pan and sauté vegetables. 4. Remove from heat and mix vegetable with cooked minced meat. Add salt and pepper. 6. Pre-heat oven. 7. Prepare pastry, Sieve flour and salt into a bowl. Rub in fat. Add enough water and bind dough together. Roll it out to shape of the pie dish (heatproof dish). 8. Put pumpkin mixture into pie dish and cover it with pastry. Cut pastry form sides and decorate the pie. Prick pre-centre pie to allow steam to escape. 9. Bake in an oven for 20–25 minutes. 10. When ready serve hot for lunch or dinner with an additional vegetable, e.g. fried cabbage.

STEAMED PUMPKIN IN COCONUT SAUCE

3 lbs (1½ kg) pumpkin

1 small onion

1 teaspoon salt

1. Wash and slice pumpkins lengthwise. 2. Peel and remove the seeds and pith. Cut as desired. 3. Wash again in salty water. 4. Put in a steaming pan, add salt and onion and steam until the pumpkin is tender but not mushy. 5. Alternatively, boil the pumpkin in very little salted water. 6. Add coconut sauce and cook for another 5-10 minutes. For sauce, see page17.

NOTE: A good pumpkin is one, which is still young. It is recognized by the greenness of its skin. There are two common type of pumpkins. The over-dark green and the green-and-cream streaky type. The former is sweeter and generally better in taste.

STUFFED PUMPKINS

1 (3 lbs or 1½ kg) pumpkin water to parboil

2 teaspoons salt

Stuffing

16 oz (500 gm) minced meat

2 teaspoons tomato puree or tomato paste

8 oz (250 gm) rice, half boiled

1 teaspoon turmeric chilli powder to taste

2 tomatoes (8 oz or 250 gm)

2 teaspoons salt

2 medium onions, chopped

2 tablespoons lemon juice

3-4 cloves of garlic, chopped

2 tablespoons oil

½ teaspoon *kotimiri* chopped

Oven temperature

R 5 (40ºF – 20ºC)

1. Wash and cut pumpkin into half, longwise. Remove seeds and all pith. 2. Parboil the pumpkin in hot salty water until the pumpkin is half-done, about 10 minutes. 3. Mix the stuffing ingredients together. 4. Remove the pumpkin from water and place on baking dish or tin. Add well-mixed stuffing and bake in a moderate oven for 1-1½ hours, or until the stuffing is cooked. 5. Serve hot or cold with mixed vegetables, other suitable types of stuffing can be including flaked fish, mixed vegetables, etc.

BUTTERED PUMPKINS

16 oz (½ kg) young pumpkins

2 oz (60 gm) butter

1 medium onion, sliced

salt to taste

1. Wash pumpkins to remove loose dirt and sand. 2. Slice, remove seeds and pith. 3. Peel and cut into even pieces. 4. Boil the pumpkins in a little salty water in which onion has been added. 5. Cook without stirring until the pumpkins are just done. 6. Drain off the remaining water, add the butter and toss carefully, so as not to break the pumpkins too much. 7. Serve as a vegetable.

NOTE: The pumpkins can be steamed instead of boiling, and this produces even better results.

PUMPKIN LEAVES WITH GROUNDNUTS

16 oz (500 gm) young pumpkin leaves

1 teaspoon turmeric

8 oz (250 gm) large tomato

1 teaspoon salt

1 large onion

1-2 green chillies

4 oz (120 gm) groundnuts finely ground

½ pt (¼ litre) water

1. Wash the leaves thoroughly to remove sand. 2. Remove the fibrous strings from the stalks. 3. Hold the leaves in bundles and shred finely. 4. Peel and slice tomatoes and onions. 5. Put shredded pumpkin leaves in little boiling salted water and cook for 10 minutes. Add onions, tomatoes, chillies and seasoning. 6. Mix groundnuts with water into a paste, add to the cooking mixture, continue coking until the pumpkin leaves and groundnuts are cooked.

NOTE: Young pumpkin leaves are the first two-to-three leaves from the growing end of a pumpkin plant. 2. Pumpkin leaves are at their best and most abundant rainy seasons.

PUMPKIN LEAVES WITH CASHEW NUTS - method 1

4 bundles pumpkin leaves

½ teaspoon curry powder

2 oz (60 gm) cashew nuts, ground

½ teaspoon turmeric

1 onion, chopped

½ green chilli

salt to taste

1 large tomato, chopped

1 oz (30 gm) fat

1. Boil the water with Salt. 2. Wash and prepare pumpkin leaves. 3. Plunge the pumpkin leaves in the boiling water for a few minutes. 4. After they change colour to dark green, remove leaves and chop up. 5. Fry the onions, add in tomatoes, curry powder, turmeric, chilli, salt and cashew nuts. 6. Add in the pumpkin leaves and simmer for 5 minutes. 7. Serve with *ugali*, rice, bananas, or cassava.

PUMPKIN LEAVES WITH CASHEW NUTS - method 2

2 bundles pumpkin leaves

1 tomato, chopped

1 oz (30 gm) cashew nuts

1 fresh chilli, chopped, roasted and crushed

½ teaspoon turmeric

1 tablespoon fat

½ teaspoon curry powder

1 onion, chopped

salt to taste

1. Wash the leaves thoroughly and finely shred. 2. Prepare the cashew nuts. 3. Prepare onions and tomatoes. 4. Boil the leaves in a very little amount of water until nearly cooked. 5. Heat the fat in a pan and fry the onions and chilli until light brown. 6. Add tomatoes and spices. Cook covered until the mixture is soft. 7. Add the pumpkin leaves, then the cashew nuts and cook for about 5 minutes. Add a little amount of water if required. 8. Serve with *ugali*, rice, or any starch dish.

PUMPKIN LEAVES IN COCONUT MILK

16 ox (500 gm) pumpkin leaves

1-2 chillies

salt to taste

1 (8 oz 250 gm) large tomato

¼ pt (1/8 litre) coconut milk

1 large onion

¼ pt (1/8 litre) water

1 teaspoon turmeric

1 oz (30 gm) fat

1. Wash the leaves thoroughly and remove sand. 2. Remove fibrous parts of the stalks. 3. Shred the leaves finely. 4. Peel and slice tomatoes and onions. 5. Put pumpkin leaves in boiling salted water cook for 10 minutes. 6. Put fat, onion, tomatoes, spices and flat flavourings in a pan and cover, bring to boil. Reduce heat and simmer until soft. 7. Add partially cooked pumpkin leaves and coconut milk. Continue cooking for 10-15 minutes or until both the vegetables and coconut milk are cooked. 8. Serve hot as a vegetable.

STUFFED PEPPER

8 large peppers

Stuffing

8 oz (¼ kg) minced meat

1 piece clove garlic, chopped

2 oz (60 gm) rice

salt and pepper to taste

2 tablespoons tomato paste or puree

4 tablespoons water of bone stock

1 teaspoon chopped parsley or *kotimiri*

1 medium onion, finely chopped

1. Wash and cut the tops off the peppers, reserve these. Remove all the seeds, as these are hot to taste. 2. Blanch the peppers in hot salted water for five minutes. 3. Soak rice in hot water for 10-15 minutes. 4. Cook both the rice and the meat separately or use leftover. 5. Mix the rest of ingredients omitting water. 6. Stuff the blanched peppers and bake uncovered in a moderate oven for 30 minutes. 7. Serve hot with a cause.

NOTE: Other vegetables which can be cooped e.g. tomatoes, marrow, potatoes, may be stuffed in a similar way with a variety of stuffing. For vegetarians use mixed vege- table or other non-meat stuffing.

MAGIMBI LEAVES (YAM LEAVES)

8 oz (¼ kg) young *magimbi* leaves

½ chilli

1 onion

½ teaspoon turmeric

salt to taste

1 tablespoon ghee or oil

1. Wash *magimbi* leaves and cut into fine shreds. 2.Boil in a little salt water till tender. 3. Chop onions. 4. Heat fat, add onions, fry until tender but not brown, seasonings and the cooked *magimbi* leaves. Continue to cook for another five minutes. 5. Serve as a vegetable with other dishes to make a balanced meal.

NOTE: *Magimbi* belongs to the yam group and grows in wet marshy land or on the edges of rives and streams and in slow moving shallow waters.

SPINACH WITH GROUNDNUTS

16 oz (½ kg or 2 bundles) spinach

1 teaspoon turmeric

1 large tomato

1-2 chillies

1 large onion

½ pt (¼ litre) water or vegetable stock

4 oz (120 gm) groundnuts,   finely ground

salt to taste

2-3 cloves garlic

1. Blanch tomatoes in hot water, peel and chop. 2. Peel and finely slice onions, chillies and garlic. 3. Put onions, tomatoes and flavourings in a pan and cook covered at low heat. 4. Remove stalks from spinach; wash thoroughly under running water if possible. 5. Mix the groundnuts with the water or stock. 6. Add to cooking onions and tomatoes and continue to simmer. 7. Blanch spinach in boiling water for ten seconds. Remove and chop finely on a board. 8. Add the spinach to the cooking mixture and continue to simmer for another five to ten minutes. 9. Serve hot as a vegetable sauce.

FRIED SPINACH

16½ kg or 2 bundles spinach

1 green chilli

1 large onion

2 oz (60 gm or 2 tablespoons) fat

salt to taste

1. Prepare the spinach by removing the tough part of the steam and washing thoroughly. 2. Blanch in hot water for a few minutes (1-2 minute). 3. Drain and chop finely. 4. Slice onion. 5. Heat fat in a pan. Add onions, chilli and fry till onions are tender. Add the chopped spinach and salt. Fry for a few minutes, lower heat and continue to cook covered until cooked but crisp. 6. Serve hot as a vegetable.

CAULIFLOWER AU GRATIN

1 (8 oz or 240 gm) small cauliflower

salt to taste

½ pt (¼ litre) white sauce of coating thickness

½ oz (15 gm) butter

1. Cut cauliflower into springs. Remove the hard leaves. Wash thoroughly in salt water. 2. Put to boil in salt water until quite tender 3. Prepare the white sauce while the cauliflower is boiling. 4. Strain the cauliflower and arrange it in a greased fireproof dish. 5. Pour the white sauce over the cauliflower and put knobs of butter on top. 6. Grill until golden brown or put into a hot oven. 7. Serve hot with a starchy dish.

CHEESE CAULIFLOWER AU GRATIN

Proceed as for cauliflower au gratin but use eggs in the sauce. Also, sprinkle the top with chopped boiled eggs.

CABBAGE ROLLS

4 cabbage leaves, well shaped

1 bunch *kotimiri*, chopped

a pinch of chilli powder to taste

6 oz (180 gm) minced meat

1 teaspoon curry powder

salt to taste.

1 sweet pepper, chopped

1 carrot, shredded

1 teaspoon tomato paste

1 large onion, chopped

2 tablespoons fat

2 cloves garlic, crushed

1 teaspoon lemon juice

1. Wash the cabbage leaves. Remove the hard middle part. 2. Prepare the stuffing – melt the fat in a pan add the chopped onions, seasonings and lemon juice and fry lightly. 3. Add the carrots, herbs, tomato paste, sweet pepper. Fry for a few minutes, then add the meat. Continue to fry until the meat changes colour, lower heat and cook until the meat is almost dry. Taste for seasonings. 4. Dip the cabbage leaves in boiling water for ten seconds. Remove. 5. Divide the meat mixture into four equal portions and place each on a leaf. 6. Roll each neatly, secure with a metal or wooden skewer or string. 7. The rolls can now be either: Fried in a little fat, or baked in a moderate oven till the cabbage leaves are well cooked and light browned on the outside and the meat cooked.

CURRIED CABBAGE

6 oz (180 gm) cabbage

1 teaspoon curry powder

1 small piece ginger

1 tomato

1 chill

2 teaspoons ghee or meat

1 onion

¼ pt (½ cup) water or meat stock

2 cloves garlic

1. Shred cabbage finely. Wash thoroughly. 2. Chop ginger, chill and garlic. 3. Peel and slice onion and tomato. 4. Heat fat in a pan, fry onion lightly. 5. Add spices and tomato; cook covered until the tomato is soft. Add washed cabbage. Stir well and fry for a few minutes. 6. Cover the pan, lower the heat and cook until the cabbage is cooked but crisp. 7. If necessary, add more water while cooking. 8. Serve hot.
NOTE: The cabbage can be steamed before adding to the sauce. Ten fry for a few minutes before serving.

BRAISED CABBAGE

8 oz (¼ kg) cabbage

3 tablespoons water

1 onion

½ teaspoon hot sauce

1 level tablespoon ghee or other fat

Salt to taste

1. Finely shred the cabbage, wash thoroughly. 2. Chop onion. 3. Melt the fat and fry the onion slightly. 4. Add the cabbage and seasonings. Lower the heat. Cook for a

few minutes (5-10 minutes). Shake the pan with the lid on occasionally. 5. Add water if necessary, otherwise continue to cook slowly until the cabbage is cooked but still crisp. 6. Serve hot.

BAMIA WITH GROUNDNUTS

16 oz (500 gm) *bamia*

4 oz groundnuts, ground

3 oz (250 gm) large tomato

1 teaspoon lime juice

½ pt (¼ litre) water

1-2 cloves garlic, chopped

salt to taste

1 large onion, chopped

1 level teaspoon curry powder

1. Wash and scrape *bamia*. Cut off both ends. Slice in half lengthwise. 2. Peel and chop tomato. 3. Put *bamia*, onion, tomato, curry powder and salt in a pan, Add ¼ pt (1/8 litre) boiling water. 4. Cook for 10-20 minutes. Add lime juice. 5. Mix groundnuts with remaining ¼ pt (⅛ litre) water. 6. Continue cooking at low heat, and stirring occasionally for another 5-10 minutes. Add more hot water if necessary. **NOTE:** The groundnuts should be roasted before grinding. This avoids lengthy cooking which tends to make the groundnuts stick and burn at the bottom of the pan.

BAMIA IN COCONUT MILK

16 oz (½ kg) *bamia*

1 green chill sliced

1 large tomato

1 teaspoon lime juice, (optional)

¼ pt (1/8 litre) coconut milk made from 1 large coconut

Salt to taste

2 large onions

¼ pt hot water

1 teaspoon turmeric

1-2 cloves garlic

1. Wash and scrape the *bamia*, cut off both ends. 2. Peel and slice onions, tomatoes and garlic. 3. Put all ingredients, except coconut milk and lime juice, in a pan, add hot water. Bring to boil, reduce heat and simmer for 10-20 minutes depending on the tenderness of the *bamia*. 4. Add lime and cook for another five minutes before adding the coconut milk. 5. Simmer for 5-10 minutes to allow the coconut milk to cook. Serve hot as a vegetable.

NOTE: To taste if bamia is not too matured, the thin tip should break off easily just by using two fingers. Lime curdles coconut milk if added at the same time . Lime or lemon juice is used to get rid of the sliminess of bamia, but it tends to bleach the green colour of the vegetable.

41

BRAISED PEAS AND CARROTS

8 oz (240 gm) shelled peas

2 teaspoonful ghee or other cooking fat

8 oz (240 gm) carrots

1 teaspoon flour

salt to taste

1 onion

hot sauce to taste

½pt (¼ litre or 1 cup) water or meat stock

1. Wash carrots and peas separately. 2. Scrape and slice carrots into rings. 3. Slice onions into thin circles. 4. Heat fat in a pan. Add onion and fry lightly. 5.Add flour, stir till cooked, but not Add carrots, peas and seasonings, then add water slowly stir-

ring to avoid lumps. 6. Simmer until vegetables are cooked and the sauce has thickened slightly. 7. Serve hot.

COOKED VEGETABLES SALAD

8 oz (240 gm) carrots

8 oz (240 gm) potatoes, peeled and diced

8 oz (240 gm) shelled peas

4 oz (120 gm) gourd, peeled and diced salt to salt to taste

1. Steam or boil vegetables with salt till tender. Potatoes are better boiled separately as they tend to cook faster and become mushy. 2. When ready add either mayonnaise sauce or tomato and onion sauce.

DRIED VEGETABLES

6 oz (180 gm) dried vegetables

1 cup coconut milk (optional)

1 large tomato

1 large onion

1 teaspoon turmeric

1 chill

2 cloves garlic

1 tablespoon oil

salt to taste

1. Wash vegetables thoroughly to remove sand. 2. Soak in little cold water for a few hours. 3. Put to boil in the water in which vegetables soaked, until soft. By now, there should be little or no liquid left. 4. Peel and finely slice tomato, onions and garlic. 5. Heat fat lightly, fry the onions, add tomato, seasonings and slowly cook covered until the tomato and onions are cooked. Add a little coconut milk if necessary. 6. Add

vegetables and coconut milk and cook gently for another 5-10 minutes Taste for salt.
7. Serve with rice, *ugali* and some meat, fish or poultry.

DRIED SPINACH

spinach, any amount

water to blanch

1. Remove spinach leaves from hard stalks. 2. Wash thoroughly. 3. Put a small amount of leaves in a pan and pour boiling water over it, turn leaves once, remove and soon as they wilt. 4. Allow leaves to drain well. 5. Repeat process for remaining spinach.
6. Spread out on clean mat and dry thoroughly before storing for future use. 7. Air from time to time.

NOTE: Blanching spinach in small quantities at a time avoids over-cooking.

DRIED KUNDE LEAVES

young *kunde* or *maharage* leaves

water for blanching

Proceed as for spinach leaves.

DRIED PUMPKINS LEAVES

young pumpkin leaves

water for blanching

1. Wash pumpkins leaves thoroughly. 2. Strip stalks to remove excess strings. 3. Shred leaves. 4. Put in a pan and pour a small amount of hot water over them. Turn until leaves wilt and turn deep green. 5. Remove leaves, drain well and spread out on a clean mat to dry. 6. Dry thoroughly before storing for future use. 7. Air dry pumpkin leaves from time to time.

4
MEAT, POULTRY AND FISH

STUFFED RICE UGALI

8 oz (240 gm) rice
¼pt (1/8lt) coconut milk
¼ pt (1/8lt) fresh milk
 a pinch of salt

For Stuffing

6 oz (180 gm) beefsteak
½ teaspoon curry powder
1 medium onion, chopped
¼ teaspoon turmeric
½ clove garlic, crushed
½ level teaspoon salt
1 teaspoon tomato paste or 1 desert spoon fat

1 small tomato, chopped

Prepare the stuffing:

Wash meat and cut into very small pieces. Boil meat in ¾ pt (3/8 pt) salted water for 1 hour or less, or until tender. When meat is ready, heat fat in a pan. Fry onions and garlic until tender but not brown. Add pieces of meat and fry over low heat for five minutes. Mix curry powder and turmeric with tomato paste. Cook these together with the meat for seven more minutes.

Prepare ugali:

Pour coconut milk in a saucepan and put to boil. Prepare smooth flour paste by mixing tow tablespoons flour with some fresh milk. When coconut milk boils, add paste and stir with a wooden spoon to avoid lumps. When mixture starts to boil again leaves it for five minutes to allow the starch grains to cook. Stir in rest of flour with a wooden spoon over a low heat for ten more minutes. Increase heat and leave the pan to stand for three minutes. Stir again for a few minutes. Add more flour if necessary. Serve the *ugali* on an oval plate, dividing it into four portions. Shape them into rounds. Make a well at centre of each round. Put equal amounts of hot stuffing inside each well. Serve the stuffed *ugali* hot with a moist vegetable.

MASHED POTATOES AND PEAS WITH MEAT

16 oz (½ kg) potatoes

1 teaspoon ghee

8 oz (¼ kg) lean meat

½ teaspoon curry powder

6 oz (180 gm) shelled peas

¼ teaspoon turmeric

1 tablespoon tomato paste

1 teaspoon salt

1. Wash and cut meat into very small, even pieces. 2. Boil it in about 1 cup of water for about ½ hour. 3. Shell the peas, wash and cook them in boiling water till soft. 4. Peel potatoes, wash and cook them in boiling water. 5. Peel and chop onion. 6. Heat ghee in a pan and fry the onion till golden brown. 7. Add cooked meat, tomato paste and all seasoning (curry, turmeric, and salt). Add remaining meat stock.
8. Mash potatoes and peas together. 9. Mix them well. Add to the meat, mash them up again. 10. Serve hot.

NOTE: This is a very good dish for expectant and nursing mothers, as well as for children, elderly people and invalids.

FRIED CABBAGE WITH MEAT

16 oz (½ kg) one small cabbage

1 small chilli or chilli powder

8 oz (¼ kg) lean beef or *kawaida*

1 onion

1 large tomato or 1 level tablespoon tomato paste

1 tablespoon cooking oil

salt to taste

½ teaspoon curry powder (optional)

a little lemon or lime juice

½ teaspoon turmeric

1. Wash and cut meat into small cubes. 2. Boil the meat in small amount of salty water until tender. 3. Shred the cabbage finely and wash thoroughly. 4. Peel onion and fresh tomatoes, if used chop both well. 5. Collect all dry ingredients add the lemon juice.
6. Put fat, tomatoes and onion in a pan and sauté lightly. Add seasonings. 7. Add well-drained cabbage, cook slowly until almost done about 10 minutes, and then add

the cooked meat plus a little stock. 8. Stir well and continue to cook for another five minutes or more. 9. Serve hot with *ugali*, rice, boiled cassava or other starchy dishes.

PLAIN NDOLO (MEAT IN YELLOW MAIZE)

1 lb (½ kg) dry pounded maize

11/2 lb (3/4 kg) goat's meat

3½ tablespoons palm oil or any cooking oil

1 lb (¾ kg) goat's meat

1 rounded teaspoon turmeric

1 onion, sliced

salt to taste

1 tomato

1. Pound the maize in a mortar or have it done at a milling factory, to remove the husks or buy ready pounded maize from flour milling factory. 2. Soak the maize overnight. Next day put to boil in a pan and cook until tender. 3. When tender, drain excessive liquid and add some oil, about 2 tablespoons. 4. Wash meat and cut into even pieces. 5. Peel onion, skin tomato and slice them. 6. Heat one tablespoon of the oil, fry the onion, tomato and add turmeric. 7. Add in the meat, fry for few minutes until the meat turns slightly brown. 8. Add enough liquid (water) and cook for approximately 45 additional minutes, until the meat is cooked. 9. Ten minutes before serving, mix the meat with the cooked maize and taste for seasonings. 10. Serve hot with a vegetable.

MEAT AND RICE ROAST

8 oz (¼ kg) rice

1 teaspoon salt

8 oz (¼ kg) lean meat or minced meat

1 tomato

1 onion

2 oz (60 gm) flour

2 eggs

2 cloves garlic

Oven temperature:

R 5(37ºF – 18ºC)

1. Wash rice and soak it. 2. Wash meat and cut into neat pieces. 3. Boil meat in salty water. 4. Boil rice in salty water until very soft. 5. Peel and chop onions very finely. Crush garlic. 6. Remove the meat from the stock and mince it finely using a mincer. Mash the rice. 7. Put the meat into a mixing bowl. Add the mashed rice, chopped onions and tomatoes, then add the flour, then the beaten eggs. 8. Using a pastry knife, mix these ingredients well and turn the mixture on a floured board. Shape into a loaf. 9. Put hot fat on a roasting tin, and place the loaf on it. 10. Bake for 30 minutes, basting occasionally. 11. When cooked, meat hot as a main dish with *mchuzi* made from the meat stock, and vegetables.

48

BEEF BIRIANI

½ lb (¼ kg) lean beef

¼ level teaspoon cardamom, ground

8 oz (240 gm) rice

¼ level teaspoon ground chilli

3 large onions

¼ teaspoon ground cinnamon

3 cloves garlic

2 tablespoon lemon juice

½ teaspoon ground coriander

4 oz (120 gm) fat

¼ teaspoon cloves, crushed

For rice

7 sticks cinnamon

1 medium chilli pepper

3 cardamoms, whole

½ teaspoon turmeric

bay leaves (optional)

salt to taste

1. Wash and cut the meat into small cubes. 2. Put the meat in a saucepan with all ground spices; coriander, cloves, cardamom, chilly and crushed garlic, some onion, plus 2 oz. fat. Lower heat and cook gently for about 15 minutes. 3. Prepare the rice for biriani. **NOTE:** The rice must be soaked for 2 hours. 4. Fill the saucepan without ¾ pint of water. Put in all the spices for beef biriani hot as a main dish. Garnish with field water to boil. Put in the rice and let it boil until it becomes partially cooked. Drain off excess water and place the rice on a tray to cool. Make the turmeric into a paste with two tablespoons hot water. 5. Mix the rice with the spice meat (use a large saucepan) plus a small portion of the onions. Fry the rest of the onions. 6. Cook for about 5 minutes then add the same liquid strained from the rice, just enough to finish cooking the rice. 7. Pour turmeric paste over the rice. 8. Lower heat, and simmer gently for about 15 minutes. Stir when necessary to avoid burning the bottom food. 9. Serve beef biriani hot as a main dish. Garnish with field onions, grilled potatoes and lemon wedges.

 49

NOTE: This is a rather oily dish and highly spiced.

KANDE WITH MEAT

4 oz (120 gm) pounded maize

½ chilli, cut into rings

6 oz (180 gm) steak, cut into cube

1 level teaspoon white pepper

1 medium tomato

2 cloves garlic, crushed

salt to taste

1 medium onion, chopped

¾ pt (3/8 litre) coconut milk

1 level teaspoon curry powder

1 tablespoon oil

1 level teaspoon turmeric

1. Soak the maize overnight. 2. Put maize to boil until tender. 3. Fry the onions and garlic, then add tomatoes, chill, curry powder, turmeric, white pepper and salt. Then add in the meat. Cook until meat is almost done. 4. Put the cooked maize in the fried meat and mix. 5. Add in coconut milk, stir for a while and simmer for 19 minutes. 6. Serve hot with vegetables.

MEAT IN VEGETABLES AND RICE RING

16 (½ kg) steak

2 large tomatoes

1 medium-sized onion

1 teaspoon lemon juice

1 clove garlic

8 oz (240 gm or about 3 medium) carrots

1 teaspoon curry powder a pinch of chill powder

¼ (4 oz) small cabbage

2 teaspoons oil

¼ teaspoon flour water

6 oz (180 gm) rice

salt to taste

1. Cut meat into small neat pieces and put to boil in little water with salt until tender.
2. Wash rice thoroughly, cook slowly in enough salty water until cooked but firm. 3. Grate the carrots, shred the cabbage and slice the onions and garlic; skin and chop tomatoes. 4. Fry the onions and garlic in one tablespoon and fat, add flour and brown; then add tomatoes. Continue to cook slowly until soft. 5. Season well (add curry powder salt and lemon juice) then add meat. 6. Cover with a plate or tin sheet and place hot charcoal over or put in a slow over to finish cooking and dry the rice. 7. Sauté the carrots and cabbage in a tablespoon of fat. Add the tomato mixture at 4. Continue to cook until the vegetables are cooked but still crisp. 8. When all is ready, arrange the meat, vegetables and rice in rings or rows in a dish or plate and serve hot. 9. Additional sauce (*mchuzi*) can be served with this dish if preferred.

MEAT WITH CASSAVA (MUHOGO)

8 oz steak

1 teaspoon lemon juice

1 medium-sized onion

½ teaspoon pepper

2 cloves garlic

1½ cup coconut milk

2 medium-sized tomatoes or 1 tablespoon tomato paste

salt to taste

¾ pt (3/8 litre) water

1 oz ghee

1 lb (½ kg) fresh cassava root

1. Wash steak and cut into large pieces. 2. Put water in a saucepan, add salt and meat. 3. Leave to boil until cooked. 4. Peel cassava, remove the pith and cut into moderately large pieces. Put to boil in salty water till half done. 5. Peel and slice onion and garlic, add to the meat. 6. Add salt and lemon juice. 7. Plunge, skin and chop the tomatoes. Add to the cooking meat. 8. Prepare the coconut milk and add to the meat. 9. Strain t he parboiled cassava and add to the meat. 10. Bring mixture to boil, stirring slowly so that the cassava does not break. 11. Cover it and leave to simmer, until the cassava is cooked thoroughly but not mushy. 12. Serve with green vegetables, e.g. spinach or fried cabbage.

MEAT WITH BEANS

4 oz (120 gm or about 1 cup) dried beans

1 oz (30 gm) ghee

1 cup coconut milk (optional)

2 cloves garlic

8 oz (¼ kg) minced meat

1 cup stock or water

1 large onion

¼ teaspoon chilli powder

2 medium sized-tomatoes

mustard seeds

1 level tablespoon tomato puree or tomato paste

salt to taste

water

1 rounded teaspoon curry powder

½ lime

1. Soak beans overnight. Skin if preferred. 2. Boil with salt until cooked about 1 hour. 3. Boil minced meat in very little water with salt and little chopped onion. 4. Peel and chop onions and garlic very finely. Skin and chop tomatoes. 5. Fry onions, garlic and mustard seeds in hot ghee until brown. Add tomatoes the then cooked meat. 6. Add tomato paste if used, seasonings, lime juice and cooked beans. Stir well. 7. Add stock or water then coconut mil if used. 8. Continue to cook, slowly until well done with thick gravy.. 9 Serve hot with rice, ugali or other starchy dish with vegetables.

MAIZE AND BEANS WITH COCONUT MILK (KANDE ZA NAZI)

8 oz (¼ kg) dry maize

1 onion

4 oz (120 gm) dry beans

2 oz (60 gm) meat

1 cup (¼lt) coconut milk

salt and pepper to taste

1. If dried beans and maize are used, soak overnight. 2. Boil maize. When half-cooked, add beans. Leave to cook until soft. 3. Chop onion and cut meat into very small pieces, add these to the mixture. Leave to cook slowly. 4. Prepare coconut milk, add to the cooking mixture. 5. Add seasoning, stir mixture and leave to simmer for about 10 minutes. 6. Taste for salt, serve hot.

MEAT WITH DENGU (LENTILS)

12 oz (360 gm) beef/steak

2 teaspoon lemon juice

4 oz (120 gm) *dengu*

Kotimiri

2 tomatoes, medium-sized

pinch ground ginger

2 tablespoons oil

1 level tablespoon tomato puree or tomato paste

salt to taste

water

1 teaspoon curry powder

onion, medium-sized

1 green chilli

1 desert spoon vinegar

1 clove garlic

1. Wash meat and cut into their strips along the meat grain. Boil in salt water with little onion until tender. 2. Wash dengu and boil until cooked. 3. Peel onions and garlic, slice very thinly. 4. Blanch tomatoes, skin and chop. 5. Fry and garlic in hot fat until light brown. Add tomatoes, boiled meat, *kotimiri*, ginger, curry powder, chili and lemon juice or vinegar. 6. Leave to simmer for 5 or more minutes. 7. Add cooked *dengu* and mix well. 8. Continue to simmer for another 5-10 minutes. 9. Taste for salt. Serve hot with vegetables and rice, *ugali*, bananas, cassava or yams

RICE, MAIZE AND MEAT STEW

3 oz (90 gm) rice

1 teaspoon curry powder

½ lb (¼ kg) lean meat

½ teaspoon turmeric

1 large tomato

¾ pt (3/8 litre) coconut milk

1 medium onion

salt to taste

1 clove garlic

1 tablespoon fat

½ lb (¼ kg) puree (pounded maize)

1 oz (30 gm) butter or margarine parsley

1. Wash and boil the puree until almost cooked. 2. Wash rice and add to the cooking maize. 3. Add ½ pt coconut milk, 1-tablespoon fat. Cook until both rice and maize are soft.

NOTE: The mixture should not be too dry when cooked. Add some more liquid if necessary. 4. Meanwhile prepare meat stew. Cut meat into small cubes. Peel and chop onions, tomatoes and garlic. Fry onions and garlic. Add tomatoes. Add meat and fry until meat changes colour. Add remaining spices plus salt. Put in ½ pt water and simmer gently for ½ hour. 5. Stir cooked maize and rice together, just enough to let rice grains get mashed into the maize. 6. Melt butter or margarine, add to rice and maize and mix well. 7. Serve hot, mixed with meat stew as a main dish or separately. 8. Garnish with parsley and grilled tomatoes.

COCONUT PILAU

4 oz (120 gm) rice

piece of cinnamon bark

3 oz (90 gm) beefsteak

salt to taste

1 tomato, chopped

½ fresh chilli

1 onion, chopped

½ pt (¼ litre) coconut milk

1 tablespoon fat

2 cloves garlic, crushed

1 cardamom pod

a few drops of lemon juice

1. Wash meat, cut into cubes and pan boil. 2. Prepare onion, tomato, and garlic.
3. Heat fat in a pan and fry onion and garlic. 4. Add tomato and spices, then meat.
5. Prepare ½pt coconut milk and add to the mixture, stir occasionally. 6. Clean and wash rice and add to meat. Cook gently until the liquid is almost dried up. 7. Finish cooking by placing a metal plate with burning charcoal on it over the pan or finish cooking in and oven, if available. 8. Serve with a vegetable or another accompaniment.

NGANDI (GOAT MEAT WITH MASHED BANANAS)

4-5 green bananas, soft type

1 pinch of ground cloves, (Optional)

8 oz (1/8 kg) goat's meat

1 ½ cup coconut milk

1 level tablespoon tomato paste or

2 tomatoes, medium sized

salt to taste

1 teaspoon turmeric or curry powder

1 green chilli

water

4 oz (120 gm) green peas shelled

Kotimiri chopped (optional)

1. Wash and cut meat conveniently large pieces. 2. Peel, and chop onions finely.
3. Boil the peas in salt water until half cooked for 10 -15 minutes. 4. Peel, scrape and cut bananas into neat pieces; wash thoroughly. 5. Boil in water till half cooked. Drain off remaining liquid. Add peas. 6. Prepare coconut milk. Add to the banana and peas mix. Bring to boil; then simmer for 10 or more minutes. Prepare meat stew. 7. Lightly

fry onions; add seasonings then tomatoes, and some water. 8. Add the meat and leave to simmer until tender. Adding more water if necessary. 9. Mash the bananas and peas well. Add the stew and mix well or serve separately.

MEAT CASSEROLE

1 lb (½ kg) goat meat

1 teaspoon curry powder

1 lb (½ kg) potatoes

½ pint stock or water

1 teaspoon ground ginger

½ level teaspoon cloves, (optional)

1 onion, chopped

salt and pepper to taste

The short crust pastry

3 oz (90 gm) flour

½ level teaspoon salt

1½ oz (45 gm) margarine or *kimbo*

2-3 tablespoons cold water

1 tablespoon oil or ghee

Oven temperature:

R 7 (45ºF – 23ºC)

1. Peel the onion and chop. 2. Wash the meat and cut into small pieces. Peel the potatoes, cut into cubes and keep in salt water. 3. Heat oil and fry onions, add all the seasonings, then add in meat. Fry until slightly brown in colour. 4. Add just enough liquid to cook the meat for about 45 minutes. 5. Make the short crust pastry and leave to cool. 6. Boil the potatoes in salty water for about 15-20 minutes, when cooked,

leave to cool. 7. Roll out the pastry to fit the top of the casserole dish (medium-sized casserole dish). 8. When the meat and potatoes are cooked and cooled, mix and fill the casserole dish. 9. Cover the casserole with the pastry and trim off the edges. 10. Make the trimmings into long pieces about one inch wide. Damp the pastry edge and put the long trims around the casserole rims. 11. Bake in a hot oven for about 15-20 minutes. 12. Serve hot with a cooked or raw vegetable salad.

BRAISED STEAK

1 lb (½ kg) steak, preferably from a tender cut

1 medium-sized onion

1½ tablespoons oil or fat

2 large tomatoes

2 teaspoons vinegar

1 teaspoon curry powder

2 teaspoons turmeric

¼ teaspoon pepper

1 teaspoon chilli powder

lemon juice

oil for shallow frying

salt to taste

1 lb (½ kg) potatoes

1. Wash and cut the meat into slices. Tenderize by beatings slightly with a meat hammer or equivalent. 2. Mix vinegar, chilli powder, salt pepper and some lemon juice. Rub this on both sides of each slice. Leave to stand marinating for 30 or more minutes. 3. Blanch peel and chop tomatoes coarsely. 4. Heat fat, fry in onions. Add the meat slices and fry on both sides. 5. Add to the cooking meat, tomatoes and the remaining spices except turmeric. 6. Cover the pan and simmer or put in slow oven until the meat is tender. 7. Prepare the potatoes until they are cooked. 8. Serve the

steak and for 7 minutes. Drain off water. Spice with lemon juice mixed with turmeric. Heat fat in a frying pan. Fry the potatoes until they are cooked. 9. Serve the steak and use the potatoes to decorate.

POUNDED MAIZE WITH MEAT

4 oz (120 gm) pounded maize

½ teaspoon curry powder

3 oz (90 gm) beefsteak

½ teaspoon turmeric

salt to taste

1 tablespoon fat

½ pint (¼ litre) coconut milk

1 onion

1 tomato, chopped

1. Soak the maize overnight. 2. Boil the maize until soft. 3. Wash and cut meat into neat cubes. 4. Boil the meat in ½ pint (¼ litre) water until cooked. 5. Prepare the coconut milk. 6. Prepare onion and tomato. 7. Heat the fat in a pan and fry the onion until light brown. Add tomato and spices and cook until soft. 8. Add the meat, then the coconut milk, stir occasionally to avoid curdling. 9. Drain maize and add to the meat, stir well and simmer for about 15-20 minutes. 10. Serve as a main dish with a vegetable.

COCO YAMS WITH MEAT

6 oz (½ kg) yam

½ teaspoon curry powder

8 oz (¼ kg) lean meat

½ teaspoon turmeric

1 large tomato or 1 tablespoon tomato paste

salt and pepper to taste

2 tablespoons cooking oil

1 large onion

1 cup coconut milk (optional)

1. Wash meat, cut into cubes. 2. Boil the meat for about ½ hour in little water. 3. Peel and cut yams into convenient, even sizes. 4. Wash them until all the sticky sap is removed. Set aside. 5. Skin and chop onion and tomato. 6. Heat oil in a pan and fry onion until light brown, then add tomato. 7. Add the cooked meat and seasonings (i.e. salt, curry powder, turmeric, pepper), cover and leave to cook for a while. Add coconut milk and yams to the meat. Keep on stirring until mixture starts to boil and thicken. Lower heat. 9. Cover and leave to cook until the yams are soft. 10. When ready serve hot, decorated with sliced tomatoes.

CHOROKO IN MEAT CURRY

4 oz (120 gm) *choroko*

1 onion

8 oz (¼ kg) meat

1 tomato or 1 teaspoon tomato paste

salt and pepper to taste

1. Boil the *choroko* until they are nearly cooked. 2. Peel and chop onion and tomato. Cut meat into small cubes. 4. Fry onion and tomato. Add meat, and cook for 15 minutes with a little liquid. 5. Add *choroko* and tomato paste, lower heat and simmer. 6. Serve with rice or *ugali*.

CHILLI FRY

8 oz (240 gm) boiled meat

½ cup milk plus

½ onion, chopped

½ cup water

1 tomato, chopped or 1 tablespoon tomato puree

1 tablespoon fat or ghee

masala

2 cloves garlic, crushed

1 teaspoon lemon juice

2 teaspoons coconut, grated

1 teaspoon turmeric

1 teaspoon *kotimiri*, chopped

salt to taste

1 teaspoon oil

1. Cut the meat into cubes. 2. Collect the masala ingredients and mix in a bowl. Add the meat cubes and leave to stand for 10-20 minutes. 3. Heat fat in a pan and fry the onions. 4. Add the spiced meat, then the tomato paste and fry for a few minutes. 5. Add the liquid, and cook until it is very thick almost dry. 6. Serve hot.

NOTE: Stock in which meat was cooked can be used instead of water.

MUTTON ORANGE STEW

½ lb (¼ kg) mutton

2 teaspoons sugar

juice of 4 large oranges

2 tomatoes

rind of ½ orange

2 large potatoes

1 tablespoon ghee or oil

2 large carrots

1. Wash and cut meat into even pieces. 2. Make the orange juice and rind from the orange. 3. Chop onion, skin tomato and slice both. 4. Peel potatoes, scrape carrots and slice both. 5. Heat the fat, fry together onion, tomatoes and some of the orange rind. 6. Add in the meat, potatoes and carrots. Add a little water to begin with and cook for about 30 minutes. Add more water if necessary. 7. Add in the orange juice, and sugar (amount of sugar depends on individual taste). 8. Cook again for about 20 minutes on low heat or until the meat is tender. 9. Serve in a deep dish garnished with the remaining orange rind. 10. Serve hot with rice, *ugali* or potatoes.

MUTTON MANGO FRY

½ lb (¼ kg) mutton cutlets

2 tomatoes or tablespoon tomato paste

1 onion sliced

salt to taste

1 clove garlic chopped

2 green mangoes

¼ teaspoon chilli powder

juice of 1 lime or lemon

1 teaspoon curry powder

1. Peel the mangoes, cut into thin, long slices and boil in just enough water to cook. 2. Peel the onion, plunge the tomatoes in hot water, skin and slice. 3. Wash meat and cut into even cubes. 4. Heat oil, fry the onion until brown and remove from the pan. 5. Add the meat into the same pan, fry the meat lightly on both sides and add in the

tomatoes. 6. Mix in t he tomatoes properly, cook for some time. 7. Return the cooked onions into the meat-and-tomatoes mixture. 8. Add the lime or lemon juice. 9. Add water a little at a time, and cook for about 30-40 minutes until the meat is cooked (keep the liquid thick). Add the mangoes. 10. Serve hot with rice or potatoes and vegetables.

MUTTON FLAN

1 lb (½ kg) mashed potatoes

4 cloves garlic, chopped

½ lb (¼ kg) boiled carrots

1/4 teaspoon pepper

2 onions chopped

1 oz (30 gm) fresh bread crumbs

1 rounded teaspoon curry powder

1 lb (½ kg) mutton or Lamb (loin), minced or finely chopped

salt to taste

Oven temperature:

R 6 (40ºF – 23ºC)

1. Wash, peel, slice and boil potatoes in salty water for 15-20 minutes. 2. Wash, scrape and slice carrots very thinly. Boil in salty water for 10 minutes. 3. Heat oil, fry the onions. Add garlic, curry powder, pepper, salt and meat. 4. Add water and cook meat for about 30-35 minutes; for minced meat, cook for 20-25 minutes. 5. Grease a flan ring. Mash the potatoes and line the tin with it. Bake blind for 10-15 minutes. 6. Fill the flan in alternate layers of meat and carrots, ending with meat on top. 7. Garnish with the breadcrumbs and leave under a hot grill for 5 minutes to brown. Garnish with some of the remaining carrots. 8. Serve hot with vegetables.

NOTE: Serve in the same dish as it is difficult to turn out the potatoes.

MUTTON CHOP IN CHUTNEY

4 mutton chops

4 oz (120 gm) breadcrumbs

1 teaspoon ginger

1½ lb (¾ kg) mashed potatoes

2 cloves garlic, chopped

oil for deep frying

1 egg

Lemon chutney (masala)

1½ lemon juice

1 clove garlic, peeled

8 bunches *kotimiri,* finely chopped

2 teaspoons salt

2 teaspoons sugar

16 green chillies

2 teaspoons jeera

1. Boil the muttonchops with ginger and garlic for about 45 minutes or until tender. 2. Peel and boil the potatoes in salt water for 15-20 minutes. 3. Grind the spices for chutney on a grinding stone or pound in a mortar. 4. Mix the ground masala with the lemon juice and sugar. Add salt to the chutney. 5. Beat the egg in small basin and pour on a plate. 6. Cover each chop with the chutney on both sides, (leaving the bone to hold). 7. Coat the chops with mashed potatoes sealing the meat and bone properly. 8. Heat the deep frying oil, test if not enough. 10. Deep fry the chops to a nice brown colour. 11. Drain off some of the oil on an absorbent piece of paper. 12. Serve hot for lunch or supper with vegetables.

MUTTON WITH NYANYA (BEAN LEAVES)

1 lb (½ kg) goat's meat

2 bunches (about ½ lb or ¼ kg) spring bean leaves (*majani ya kunde*)

1 onion, chopped

4 oz (120 gm) groundnuts, finely pounded

salt to taste

½ level tablespoon ghee or oil

1. Wash the meat and cut into even cubes. 2. Heat oil, fry onion and meat until brown in colour. 3. Add enough water to cover the meat. 4. Cook for about 45 minutes, adding more water if necessary. 5. Cut the bean leaves from their stalks and wash in cold salty water. 6. Blanch, then chop, the leaves and add into the cooking meat. 7. Sprinkle the crushed groundnuts on to of the bean leaves, cook the mixture for about 15 to 20 extra minutes, or long enough to cook the vegetable. 8. Add more liquid if necessary, mix well and taste for salt. 9. Serve hot in a deep dish with ugali or rice.

RICE AND MUTTON BIRIANI

1 lb (½ kg) rice

1 coconut

1 lb (½ kg) meat

3 tomatoes, sliced

3 tablespoons ghee heaped

1 garlic bulb, sliced

4 rounded teaspoons curry powder

5 large lemons for juice or s tablespoons vinegar

2 rounded teaspoons turmeric

salt and pepper to taste

3 large onions, thinly sliced

1. Wash meat, remove gristles and cut into very thin strips. 2. Peel onions and slice them. 3. Plunge tomatoes in hot water skin and slice them. 4. Squeeze the lemon juice into a bowl, removing all the seeds. 5. Peel and chop garlic. 6. Mix the meat with all seasonings, tomatoes, onions and lemon juice into the cooking pan. 7. Add a little water to start with and cook for about 45-55 minutes, until the meat is tender. 8. Add more water if necessary, stirring with a wooden spoon. 9. Prepare enough coconut milk for cooking the rice. 10. Clean the rice and leave for a few minutes in cold water. 11. Boil the coconut milk with salt, ad the rice and cook for about 20 minutes or until the rice is almost cooked. 12. Cover the pan with a plate or pan cover and put charcoal on top to finish the cooking and dry the rice. 13. Serve the meat and rice in alternate layers. 14. Garnish with sliced tomato. Serve hot as a special dish for the day, accompanied with vegetables or salad.

NOTE: When the meat is cooked it should have very thick sauce in it.

CASHEW NUT ROAST

66

4 oz (120 gm) cashew nuts, roasted

a pinch of chilli

4 oz (120 gm) minced meat

1/8 pt milk

1 medium onion

½ level teaspoon salt

½ teaspoon curry powder

1 teaspoon fat

1 egg

Over temperature:

R 4(35ºF – 17ºC)

1. Peel and chop onion. 2. Mince cashew nuts or chop finely. 3. Melt fat in a pan, fry onion, add meat, curry powder, chilli and salt and fry lightly for 3 minutes. 4. Remove meat, mix with cashew nuts. Beat the egg, mix with milk. 5. Put everything in a large bowl and mix together. 6. Grease ½ lb. bread tin. Pour mixture in tin, roast in moderately hot oven for 45 minutes. 7. When done, turn onto a plate and serve.

6 oz (180 gm or 1 cup) rice

1 tablespoon corn flour or wheat flour

2 slices fresh ginger, if available

1 tablespoon soy sauce ,

salt to taste

2 teaspoons turmeric

1-2 cloves garlic

1 onion

1 tablespoon oil

1 lb (½ kg) minced meat

egg, beaten

1. Soak the rice in sufficient water, adding salt and turmeric for 2-3 hours. Then drain. 2. Mince or chop finely the onion, garlic and ginger, then mix with meat, corn flour, salt, oil and soy sauce and beaten egg. 3. Shape the above mixture into small balls 2-3 cm. (1-1¼ inches) diameter and roll them in the rice grains, pressing so that the rice grains coat the meatballs. 4. Spread the remaining rice on the plate in which the meatballs are to be steamed. 5. Arrange the meatballs on plate, stand the plate on a tin inside of a pan of boiling water. 6. Steam covered for 20-30 minutes or until cooked. Serve hot with rice and vegetables.

NOTE: The balls could be cooked in a tightly covered dish in a low oven, and extra liquid added if necessary.

STEAMED MEAT CUPS

3 oz (90 gm) flour

1½ oz (45 gm) sugar

1½ oz 45 gm) fat or margarine

1 beaten egg and 4 tablespoons of cold water

1 rounded teaspoon baking powder

3 teaspoons honey, (optional)

3 oz (90 gm) minced meat

1. Cook the minced meat for a few minutes in a very small amount of water. Cook until almost dry. 2. Prepare a pan of boiling water or a steamer. 3. Prepare the mixture. Sieve flour and baking powder into a bowl. Rub in fat with the finger tips. Add sugar and the boiled minced meat. Add the beaten egg and water, mixing with a pastry knife into a dropping consistency. Grease heat-proof cups, add honey if used, and put equal amounts into each cup. 4. Cover the cups with grease-proof paper and tie well with a piece of string. 5. Cut off the hanging pieces of the paper. 6. Steam for 1 hour, adding more water into the pan until the mixture is cooked. 7. Test for doneness with a skewer or pierce with a knife. 8. Serve hot or cold for a snack.

VERMICELLI WITH MEAT

4 oz (120 gm) vermicelli

1 oz (30gm) fat

3 oz (90 gm) beef steak, minced

½ chilli, cut into rings

½ teaspoon curry powder

1 tomato

½ teaspoon turmeric

1 onion, chopped

a pinch of nutmeg

1. Boil the vermicelli for 5 minutes and drain the water off. Set aside. 2. Fry the onion and tomato. Add in curry powder and turmeric. 3. Add in meat and fry for a while. Cover and cook until the meat is done. 4. Add in the vermicelli and mix. 5. Serve hot with vegetables.

CURRIED MINCED MEAT

6 oz (180 – 240 gm) minced meat

½ tablespoon tomato paste or tomato puree

2 tomatoes, skinned and chopped

½ cup water

1 onion, chopped

1 teaspoon turmeric or curry powder

2 cloves garlic, chopped

1 bunch herbs *kotimiri*, chopped

1 teaspoon lemon juice

1 tablespoon oil

½ chilli, chopped

 salt to taste

1. Heat the fat in a pan and fry the onion and garlic using a metal spoon to prevent sticking. 2. Add all seasonings, then tomato paste and lemon juice. 3. Add meat and stir for a few minutes, until the mixture bubbles. 4. Reduce heat and simmer with lid on until the meat is cooked.

NOTE: Add water if need be, but not otherwise. 5. Taste for salt and serve hot.

MEAT CINNAMON HEADS

(Makes 20-24 meat cinnamon heads)

2 rounded teaspoon ground cinnamon

½ lb (¼ kg) goat's meat (leg)

1 garlic chopped clove

1 rounded teaspoon salt

Short crust pastry

3 oz (90 gm) flour

½ level teaspoon salt

1½ oz (45 gm) fat or

2-3 tablespoon cold water

margarine or mixture of both

Oven temperature:

R 7(45º F – 23º C)

1. Boil the cut meat in water with one teaspoon ground cinnamon, salt and chopped garlic for about 45 minutes or until cooked. 2. Make the short crust pastry. Sift the dry ingredients together into a bowl. Rub the fat into flour until the mixture looks like fine breadcrumbs. Add enough water to make soft dough, mixing with a pastry knife. Bind the mixture together with the fingers. Leave the pastry to cook. 3. When the meat is coked, dry well, cut into even small and leave to cool. 4. Roll out the pastry into a circle. 5. Using cutters of 3 inches and 1½ inches in diameter, cut the pastry into circles of 3 inches and 1½ inches. 6. Grease two patty tins. 7. Line the tins with the 3 inches pastry circles; add the pieces of meat into each circle. 8. Wet the edges of the pastry in the patty tins. 9. Cover with the small 1½ inches pastry rounds, making sure the meat pieces are properly covered. Seal the edges and press into heads. 10. Mix the remaining one teaspoon of cinnamon with one tablespoon of cold water.

11. Using an egg brush, glaze the heads with the cinnamon mixture making sure the brushing liquid is not too wet. 12. Bake in a hot oven. 13. Serve hot or cold as a snack.

MEAT AND DHAL (LENTIL) CURRY

½ lb (¼kg) lean beef

1 medium onion

4 oz (120 gm) lentils

¼ level teaspoon chilli

1 medium tomato

salt to taste

1 teaspoon tomato paste

1 clove garlic

1 teaspoon curry powder

1 tablespoon fat

½ teaspoon turmeric

1 pt (½ litre) water

1. Put the lentils to boil in 1 pt. water. 2. Peel and chop the tomatoes, onions and garlic. 3. Wash and cut the meat into small cubes. 4. Melt 1-tablespoon fat, add onions and crushed garlic. 5. Add tomatoes, tomato paste and fry till soft, add meat and fry until the meat changes colour. 6. Add the cooking lentils over the meat. Lower heat and simmer gently for 1 hour. 7. Serve hot with rice, *ugali*, potatoes.

BEEF KABABS

6 oz (180 gm) small cubes of meat, tender cut

1 teaspoon *kotimiri*, chopped

2 slices bread

1 green chilli, finely sliced

1 clove garlic, crushed

1 pinch ground clove

1 onion, chopped

1 pinch ground cinnamon

1 teaspoon curry powder

salt to taste

1 tablespoon flour to coat

fat for deep frying

small amount water or milk

1. Soak bread in little water or milk. 2. Mix meat well with all other ingredients except flour, leave to stand for a few minutes. 3. Squeeze out liquid from the bread, add bread to the meat mixture, and mix well. 4. Form 16 small meatballs and shape between the palms of your hands. 5. Heat the fat in a fryer or frying pan; fry the balls slowly until cooked and golden brown. 6. Serve hot or cold for snacks or packed meals.

72

MEAT SAMBUSAS

4 oz (120 gm) flour

water to make stiff dough

a pinch of salt 2 tablespoons oil

Filling

4 oz (120 gm) minced meat

2 green chillies, chopped

2 cloves garlic, crushed

1 bundle *kotimiri*, chopped

2 large onions, finely chopped

1 teaspoon salt

1 pod cardamom seeds, crushed

oil for deep frying

1. Make the pastry as follows: Sift the flour into a bowl. Add salt. Make into a stiff dough with water. 2. Make the filling as follows: Cook the meat, onions and garlic in a pan until the meat is dry. Add salt and the remaining ingredients for flavouring and seasoning, mix well. Leave to cool. 3. Make the pastry cases as follows: Divide the pastry into 4 equal portions. Roll each piece into an even circle of about 4 inches diameter. Spread cooking oil evenly over each piece. Using a sieve, sprinkle a very thin layer of flour over each round. Place two rounds on top of one another, floured sides facing. Repeat the process so that there is only one round left, with a pile of circles. Gently roll out the pile of circles into a large round of about 8-9 inches (22 cm) in diameter, or the size of a large chapatti. During this final rolling, turn the pastry over and roll out. This keeps the circles the same size. Mildly heat a heavy frying pan, girdle or chapatti pan (*kikaango cha chapati*). Lightly fry the chapatti on both sides without fat, until the flour is set and NOT browned. Leave to cool slightly. Cut the set pastry into 3 even strips. Peel these pastry strips to obtain 12 thin strips. The layers were pastry and fill formed when placing the rounds one on top of the other. Make a cone with each strip of them with a tablespoon of the meat filling. 4. Close the top with the flap of pastry sticking out, and stick down with a little flour paste. 5. Fry in fairly hot fat until golden brown. 6. Drain off excessive fat and serve with lemon wedges.

NOTE: The flour paste can be made from mixing on tablespoon flour with water to from a thick paste.

MEAT AND VEGETABLE PANCAKE ROLLS

Make 6 Pancake Rolls

Butter

4 oz (120 gm) plain flour pinch of salt

1 egg

½ pt (¼lt) water

Filling

2 oz (60 gm) minced meat, chicken or prawns

1 green pepper

 a pinch of ground ginger

4 oz (120 gm) shelled peas, *kunde* or *mbaazi*

1 teaspoon *kotimiri*, chopped

½ tablespoon ghee

4 oz (120 gm) spinach, chopped

 salt to taste

1 medium-sized carrot

fat for deep frying

1 medium-sized onion

To make the batter

Sift flour and salt into a bowl. Make a well in the centre. Break egg, beat it up and mix it with water. Pour the mixture in the well and gradually stir in flour to a pouring consistency. Cover with a clean tower and keep in a cool place for 1 hour.

To prepare the filling

Wash and scrape the carrot. Dice it up into very small pieces. Wash the *kunde* and cook them in boiling salty water until tender. Add the carrots in the same pan to cook with the green *kunde*.

Wash and chop the spinach very finely. Fry onion mixture, then add minced meat. Chop onion, green pepper and *kotimiri* and mix well. Add spinach, salt and all other spices (ground ginger, *kotimiri*, pepper). Add cooked *kunde* and carrots and mix well. Taste for seasoning, re-season if necessary. Lower heat and leave to cook till fairly dry. Leave to cool. 3. Oil the frying pan (a heavy-based one is very suitable) very lightly and get it a bit hot. 4. Pour batter on the hot frying pan and move from side to side until the bottom is completely covered. Raise the heat and cook pancake on one side only. 5. When cooked, put on a plate. 6. Repeat the process until all pancakes are cooked. 7. Put a tablespoon of the filling on one-half of each pancake and roll over. Seal edges with flour paste. 8. Heat oil in a deep frying pan and deep fry filled pancakes until golden brown. 9. Drain them on an absorbent paper. 10. Serve with wedges of lemon.

NOTE: These are good for snacks, party, etc.

BALL CURRY

½ lb (¼ kg) minced meat

2 tablespoon ghee or oil

2 large onions, finely chopped

2 big tomatoes or 1 tablespoon tomato paste

1 piece fresh ginger, chopped

½ dried coconut grated

4 pieces garlic, finely chopped

1 slice stale bread

1/2 cup of water

2 tablespoons coriander powder

a pinch of kotimiri, chopped

2 teaspoons garam masala

oil for deep frying

2 teaspoons jeera

salt to taste

2 green chillies

1 beaten egg

2 red chillies

1 tablespoon seasoned flour

1 teaspoon turmeric

1. Prepare all the seasonings by chopping very finely or grinding on a stone or pounding in a mortar until very fine. 2. Make the garam masala by grinding the ingredients on a grinding stone or pounding in a mortar. 3. Mix two teaspoons of garam masala with the other seasonings in the main recipe. 4. Mix the minced meat with the ground seasonings. Add salt. 5. Knead the mixture well. 6. Soak the slice of breads in water. 7. Squeeze out water from bread and mix with the seasoned meat, knead again until the bread is well mixed. 8. Beat the egg in a small basin, put the seasoned flour on a plate. 9. Form the meatballs, coat with the seasoned flour then beaten egg. 10. Heat the oil, test with a cube of the minced meat if hot enough. 11. Deep fry the balls for about 20 minutes until golden brown and cooked. 12. Drain off some of the oil on an absorbent paper and leave in a warm place. 13. Skin the tomatoes and slice them. 14. Heat two tablespoons of oil, fry the remaining garam masala and the tomatoes for about 5 minutes. 15. Add the water and simmer for about 10 minutes, until the tomatoes are cooked. The sauce should be thick when ready. 16. Serve the balls on a plate with the sauce round it sprinkled with grated coconut.

MINCED MEATBALLS

8 oz (240 gm) minced meat

a pinch chopped herbs *kotimiri*

1 onion, finely chopped

½ beaten egg

2 cloves garlic, crushed

1 teaspoon salt

1 teaspoon curry powder

fat for shallow frying

For coating

2 tablespoons dried breadcrumbs

½ beaten egg

1. Heat a little fat in a pan and fry the onions until tender. Leave to cool. 2. Mix the meat with all the other ingredients in a bowl. Add the onions, and mix well until the mixture sticks together. 3. Form the mixture into 4-6 balls. 4. Coat each ball first with beaten egg then roll tin breadcrumbs. 5. Heat the fat in a frying pan and fry the meatballs gently until they are cooked and golden brown. 6. Serve hot or cold for snacks.

FRIED LIVER

6 oz (180gm) fresh liver

1 teaspoon lemon juice

1 teaspoon curry powder

salt to taste

1 tablespoon oil

1. Wash and skin the liver with the tip of a sharp knife. 2. Cut into neat even-sized pieces, removing any gristle. 3. Mix the other ingredients together. 4. Add the mixture

to the liver and leave to stand for 10 minutes. 5. Heat a frying pan and fry in the liver. 6. Stir the liver until it changes colour. Then lower the heat and fry gently until cooked. If the liver shows signs of drying up before it is cooked; cover with a lid and continue to cook until ready. 7. Serve hot with cooked vegetables. Well-cooked livers should show signs of blood when cut through.

CURRIED LIVER

8 oz (240 gm) liver

1 teaspoon curry powder

1 onion, chopped

2 teaspoons lemon juice

2 cloves garlic, chopped

a pinch chill powder

1 tomato, chopped

1 level tablespoon ghee or other fat

1 teaspoon turmeric

salt to taste

1 teaspoon *kotimiri*, chopped

1 cup water

1. Wash, skin and cut liver into even-sized pieces. 2. Heat the fat in a pan. 3. Fry the onions, *kotimiri* and garlic, lightly. 4. Add the seasonings, lemon juice and tomatoes, and let them cook for a few minutes. 5. Add the liver, then water. Bring to a boil.
6. Lower heat, cover pan and cook for 20 minutes or until the liver is cooked. 7. Taste for seasoning and serve hot.

LIVER AND VEGETABLE FRY

8 oz (¼ kg) ox liver

2 oz (60gm) fat or ghee

¼ small cabbage

1 clove garlic

1 medium onion

1 medium tomato or 1 level tablespoon tomato paste

1 teaspoon lemon juice

¼ teaspoon curry powder

salt to taste

2 medium-sized fresh carrots

water

1. Shred and wash the cabbage. 2. Wash, scrape and grate the carrots. 3. Put a little water in a saucepan, add in salt, bring to boil. 4. Add in the vegetables. Leave to boil until half-cooked. 5. Wash the liver skin and cut into moderately small pieces. 6. Peel and chop the onion and garlic finely. 7. Blanch, skin and chop the tomato. 8. Heat fat in a saucepan, add in onion and garlic. Fry until fairly tender. 9. Add in curry powder, pepper salt and lemon juice. 10. Add in the tomatoes and fry until fairly tender. 11. Add in the liver and fry until done, but not dry. 12. Add in the boiled vegetables and fry for 5 minutes. 13. Serve with mashed potatoes or rice.

LIVER SNACKS

½ lb (¼ kg) cooked liver

small sticks, if possible

1 egg

fat for deep-frying

3 tablespoons flour

salt and pepper to taste

1 tablespoon milk

1. Cut the liver into even cubes, season with some salt and pepper. 2. Make a coating batter with egg, milk and flour. Sieve the flour into a bowl. Make a well at the centre and add the egg and milk. Starting from the centre stir with a wooden spoon until all the flour is in corporate and the mixture is smooth. 3. Coat the liver with the batter; holding each with a stick. 4. Fry in deep fat until golden brown. 5. Drain and serve as snack.

COCONUT CHICKEN

1 kg chicken joints, broiler or boiler

2 large onions, sliced

2-3 cloves of garlic, chopped

1 tablespoon ghee or other fat

1 teaspoon turmeric

2 teaspoons flour

1 tablespoon tomato paste

½ pt (¼ litre) water or stock

1 large tomato

½ pt (¼ litre) coconut milk

a pinch of chilli powder or small fresh chilli

1 teaspoon salt

½ teaspoon *kotimiri*, chopped

1. Coat jointed chicken with flour. 2. Fry onions, garlic, add salt, tomatoes paste, turmeric, herbs and fresh tomato. 3. Add jointed chicken. Fry for another 2-3 minutes or until chicken has changed colour. 4. Stir occasionally. Cook longer for broiler chicken. 5. Add coconut milk and a simmer for another 30 minutes. 6. Serve hot with a starchy dish and vegetables.

KUKU PAKA

½ roasting chicken (¾ kg) or 1¼ lb)
1 tablespoon fat

Coconut sauce

1 large tomato
1 pt coconut milk
1 large onion, chopped
½ teaspoon turmeric
1 tablespoon lemon juice
1 teaspoon fat
½ teaspoon salt

Masala for chicken (spices)

1 teaspoon ground ginger
1 teaspoon turmeric
1 level teaspoon salt
1 teaspoon oil
A pinch of chilli powder
½ teaspoon curry powder
3-4 cloves garlic, crushed

Oven temperature:

R 6 (42°F – 21°C)

1. Wash and dry chicken. 2. Prepare masala by mixing the masala ingredients together, brush over chicken, and for about 15-20 minutes. 3. Heat fat in roasting tin or dish. Add spiced chicken. Bake for 20-30 minutes, basting occasionally. 4. Cover

and cook till tender. 5. Meanwhile prepare sauce. Melt fat. Add onions and spices, lemon juice peeled and chopped tomato. 6. Add coconut milk. Stir frequently until the milk thickens then add flour mixed with liquid to further thicken the sauce. Serve chicken and pour sauce over it.

CHICKEN AND PUMPKIN FRY

breast of one boiled chicken

1 tablespoon fat

2 cups pumpkin leaves boiled

1 cup coconut milk

1 tomato, chopped (optional)

¼ onion, chopped

2 teaspoons curry powder,

salt to taste

1. Cut the chicken into cubes. 2. Heat the fat in a pan, fry the onions, garlic and then the tomatoes. 3. Add the seasonings and continue to cook until the tomato is tender. 4. Add the coconut milk, then the chicken meat. 5. Cook until the liquid thickens and almost dry. 6. Add the cooked pumpkin leaves and continue to cook for 3-4 minutes. 7. Serve hot with a starchy dish.

CHICKEN AND BANANA CAKES

3 green bananas

curry powder

1 green chilli

12 oz (360 gm) chicken meat from carcass or left-over chicken

¼ teaspoon chilli powder

oil for deep frying

a little mint

1 egg

2 teaspoons lemon juice

1 teaspoon flour

2 cloves garlic,

salt to taste

Batter

2 tablespoons flour

¼ pint (1/8 litre) water

pinch of salt

1. Put water in the saucepan, add chicken and boil until cooked. 2. Peel bananas and scrape. 3. Slice the bananas lengthwise, and then cut into fairly small pieces. 4. Wash thoroughly with warm water to remove sap. 5. Put to boil with little water until thoroughly cooked. 6. Peel garlic and chop finely. 7. Chop the mint and green chilli. 8. Chop the chicken meat very finely or mince. 9. Mash the bananas well. 10. Add in the garlic, mint, pepper, salt, lemon juice, curry powder and mix well. Then add beaten egg and flour to bind. 11. Divide the ball into 10 equal portions. 12. Using hands, make each portion into a ball and flatten it into a round cake of ¼ inches thick. 13. Prepare the batter by mixing flour, salt and water into a thick paste fist, then add remaining water and mix well. 14. Dip each of the cakes into the batter. 15. Meanwhile heat the fat for deep frying until quite hot. 16. Fry coated cakes in hot fat until golden brown. 17. Serve hot or cold.

BEANS WITH MINCED CHICKEN

8 oz (24 gm or 1½ cup) beans

½ pint (¼ litre) coconut milk

2-3 cloves garlic

1 tablespoon lemon juice

1 large onion, pilled and chopped

2-3 tablespoons fat or oil

1-2 large tomatoes, peeled and chopped

½ pint chicken stock or water

1 tablespoon tomato paste

salt to taste

2 teaspoons curry powder

4-6 oz (120 gm) cooked chicken, chopped or minced

1. Boil beans till tender but with little or no water left. 2. Fry onions, tomato, lemon juice, seasonings, and tomato paste. Add stock and cook for 3-5 minutes. 3. Add cooked beans, coconut milk and chopped chicken. 4. Simmer for 10-15 minutes. Serve hot with a starch dish and green vegetables.

ROAST CHICKEN

1 (1¼ - 1½ kg) roasting chicken

3-4 cloves garlic, crushed

2-3 tablespoons oil or 2-3 oz (60-90 gm) fat

1 teaspoon salt

1 teaspoon curry powder or turmeric

1 tablespoon lemon juice (optional)

2 small onions

Oven temperature:

R (42ºF – 21ºC)

1. Thaw chicken thoroughly if frozen, or clean, then wash both inside and outside. 2. Mix flavorings, lemon juice and one-tablespoon oil. 3. Brush the chicken with the mixture both inside and outside. Put peeled whole onion inside the chicken with

the giblets. Keep the legs in position through the vent. 4. Leave to stand for 10-15 minutes, meanwhile heat the rest of the fat in the oven in the roasting tin till hot. 5. Put the dressed chicken to roast in the tin face down, so that the breast meat does not dry up. Allow 15-20 minutes per ½kg, plus 15 minutes more. 6. For the last 15 cooking minutes, turn the chicken onto its back for the breast to brown. 7. Serve hot with other dishes or cold in a salad.

CHARCOAL-GRILLED CHICKEN WITH TOMATO SAUCE

20 oz (1¼ kg) broiler chicken

3 tablespoons oil

1 teaspoon turmeric

Kotimiri, chopped

8 oz (¼ kg) cassava root

salt to taste

2 cloves garlic

1 green chilli

tomato and onion sauce

1 teaspoon curry powder

2 teaspoons lemon juice

1. Prepare the chicken and joint into required pieces, 8-12. 2. Peel and chop green chilli and garlic. Grind using a rolling pin. 3. Put 2 tablespoons of oil in a bowl. Add ground garlic, *kotimiri*, turmeric, curry powder, salt, lemon juice and mix well. 4. Rub the mixture on to the chicken joints,, making sure all parts get the seasoning. Leave to stand for 40-60 minutes. 5. Put the chicken joints on to hot charcoal grill, leave pieces to grill, turning them from time to time. 6. Peel the cassava, wash, dry and fry into chips. 7. Cut through one chicken thigh with a knife to see if the meat is cooked. 8. When done, remove the chicken joints from the grill and put in a serving dish.

Keep it in a warm place so that it does not get cold. 9. Serve the chicken with tomato and onion sauce, decorated with cassava chips.

MAIZE IN CHICKEN CURRY

4 oz (120 gm) pounded maize

½ dessert spoon tomato paste

8 oz (240 gm or ½ small) chicken, jointed

1 clove garlic, crushed

1 medium onion, chopped

½ dessertspoon curry powder

1 level teaspoon salt

½ pint coconut milk

1 teaspoon flour

½ oz (15 gm) fat

1. Wash and boil the maize in two pints of water until soft. This takes 1½-2 hours. 2. Mix salt flour and curry powder. Coat the chicken with this mixture. Leave to stand. 3. Heat fat and fry the onions and garlic. Add tomato paste and coated chicken. Fry over low heat for 10 minutes. Stir in coconut milk. 4. When maize is ready drain off any remaining liquid. Add the maize to the cooking mixture and simmer for about half an hour. 5. Serve as a main dish accompanied with vegetables.

NOTE: Water or fresh milk can be used instead of coconut milk.

CHICKEN BIRIANI

½ (about ½ kg or 16 oz) roasting chicken, jointed

8 oz (240 gm) rice, washed and soaked in water for 2 hours

Masala for chicken

2 oz (60 gm) fat

¼ teaspoon ground cloves

2 large onions, chopped

a pinch of ground cardamom

2 oz (60 gm) fat

a pinch of chilli powder

5 cloves garlic, crushed

¼ teaspoon ground cinnamon

½ teaspoon ground coriander

2 teaspoons lemon juice

Spices for rice

4 sticks cinnamon

¼ teaspoon turmeric

2 pods cardamoms

salt to taste

½ teaspoon black pepper corns

1. Wash the chicken and put it aside. 2. Fry onions in about two tablespoons fat till crisp and brown. Divide them into two equal portions. Crush one portion thoroughly and mix it in with all spices for the chicken masala. Spice the chicken with masala. Leave to stand for a while, and then fry in 2 oz fat. 3. Preparing the rice for biryani. Take a large saucepan, fill it three parts full with water about 1½ pint (¾ litre). Put in the spices for rice together with salt to taste. 4. When the water has boiled put the rice. When the rice is half cooked, drain through a sieve, but do not remove the spices from the rice. 5. Mix turmeric into 1 teaspoon of hot water. 6. When the rice has been drained, put it over the chicken in a large saucepan together with the remaining portion of the fried onions. Pour over melted fat and over this the turmeric mixture. 7. Add a little hot water, cover the pan, bring to boil, after that, lower the heat and simmer for 1½ hours, or until the rice is cooked but not soggy. This dish can be

garnished with sliced, boiled eggs. It can be served wit other accompaniments, too, such as vegetable salads, fried cabbage and grilled tomatoes.

BRAISED PINEAPPLE CHICKEN

1 (about 1 kg or 2 lbs) chicken

1 teaspoon curry powder

1 lb (½ kg) yams, carrots, or other thick sliced vegetables

½-pint (¼ litre) pineapple juice, unsweetened

1 large onion, chopped

salt pepper to taste

3 tablespoons oil or ghee

Oven temperature

R 7(45ºF – 23ºC)

1. Peel the vegetables, cut into thick slices and keep in cold, salty water. 2. Cut the chicken into 4 pieces. 3. Heat oil, fry the onion and the other seasonings. 4. Add in the meat and fry on both sides until the meat turns brown. 5. Remove the meat from the pan and keep on the plate, then sautee the vegetables for a few minutes. 6. Return the meat in the pan with vegetables carefully arranged at the bottom. 7. Add the pineapple juice, then enough water to cover the vegetables. 8. Cover the pan with a tightly fitting lid. Time allowed for braising is 15 to 20 minutes for each half kilo, plus 15 to 20 minutes extra. 9. Cook the meat on low heat for about 35 minutes, 2/3 of the total cooking time, adding more liquid if necessary. 10. Remove pan from heat, remove the lid and finish coking in hot oven for 15 minutes. 11. Serve hot with some more vegetables. 12. The vegetables may be served separately.

GOURDS (MAMUMUNYA CHICKEN BREAST)

1 chicken breast, broiler or boiler

½ pt coconut milk, (optional)

1½ lb (¾ kg) young gourds

1 large onion

2 teaspoons flour

1 large tomato

1-2 chillies to taste

2-3 cloves garlic

1 teaspoon turmeric

½ bundle *kotimiri* (fresh herbs)

1 teaspoon fat

1 lime

salt to taste

1. Peel, slice onion, tomato and garlic. Chop *kotimiri*. 2. Wash, peel and evenly slice gourds, removing excessive seeds. Keep in salt water. 3. Heat the fat, fry onion, add chillies and other seasonings, lemon juice and herbs. Add tomatoes. 4. Remove flesh from chicken breast and cut it into small pieces. 5. Add chicken and gourds to the tomato and onion. Fry for 2-5 minutes. Lower heat and cook covered for 20-30 minutes. 6. Add coconut milk. 7. Make a paste of flour and a little coconut milk and add to the pan. Continue to simmer until both meat and gourds are tender. 8. Serve hot with a starchy dish. **NOTE:** If the chicken used is an old, tough one, it should first be boiled until almost tender then remove from breastbone and cut up into small pieces.

HOW TO PREPARE FRESH FISH

For all types of fish

choose fresh fish.
remove the insides and wrap in paper before throwing away.
wash with plenty of water or under running tap water.

For scaly fish

line the surface (table top etc.) with paper.
scale the fish with the back of knife, starting from the tail towards the head.
wrap the scales in paper before throwing away.
rinse the fish and use as required.

FRIED FISH FILLET

2 fillets of fish
a pinch of paper
1 tablespoon flour
fat for shallow frying
a pinch of salt

1. Mix the flour, salt and pepper. 2. Wipe the fillets with clean cloth to dry. 3. Coat the fish on both sides with the seasoned flour. 4. Heat the fat until hot. 5. Quickly fry the fish on sides, then lower heat and fry until cooked and golden brown. 6. Serve decorated with lemon crescents or butterflies.

FISH MAKANDE (MAIZE)

1 lb (½ kg) fresh fish (*nguru*)
1 dessertspoon tomato puree or 1 tomato

½ cup pounded maize

2 teaspoons lemon juice

2 oz (60gm) fat or ghee

kotimiri, chopped

1 onion

salt to taste

1 teaspoon turmeric

½ teaspoon rye, (optional)

2 cloves garlic

water

1. Soak the pounded maize overnight. 2. Put the maize in a saucepan, add water and boil until cooked. 3. Wash and boil the fish for abut 10 minutes until cooked. 4. Flake the fish and remove bones if any. 5. Peel and slice onion and garlic thinly. 6. Heat fat in a saucepan, add rye, onion, garlic and fry until light brown. 7. Add in tomato puree, pepper and turmeric. 8. Add in the lemon juice, salt and flaked fish. 9. Pour in the maize and mix well. 10. Cover and leave to simmer for 7-10 minutes. 11. Serve with fried cabbage or green vegetables.

GRILLED NGURU WITH SAUCE

1 lb (½ kg) fish (*nguru*)

kotimiri

2 large tomatoes or 2 dessert spoons tomato puree

lemon juice

1 tablespoon turmeric

pinch of herbs, (optional)

salt to taste

green chilli

1 tablespoon oil

1 clove garlic

1 large onion

1. Cut the piece of *nguru* into 4. Wash and remove the outer black skin. 2. Grind garlic and green chilli. 3. Mix oil with chilli, garlic, and turmeric and lemon juice. Add in salt. 4. Rub the mixture on the fish a steak, making sure it is well distributed on all sides. 5. Put the fish on a grill pan (removing the wire). 6. Grill fish under moderate heat so that it is not burnt. 7. Turn both sides so that both sides get brown. 8. Peel and slice onion thinly. 9. Blanch, skin and chop tomatoes. 10. Warm fat in a saucepan, fry onions until tender. 11. Add tomatoes and cook covered until soft. 12. Add herbs and a little salt, plus chopped *kotimiri* and a little lemon juice. 13. Leave mixture to simmer for 5 minutes with the pan covered. 14. Put fish in a serving dish and pour the sauce on the fish. 15. Serve with potatoes or rice and a green vegetable.

CHARCOAL ROAST FISH

2 large fresh fish (*changu*)

2 tomatoes or 1 level tablespoon tomato paste

2 medium onions

½ lime

3 tablespoon oil

½ teaspoon pepper

salt to taste

1 clove, (optional)

1 ½ cup thick coconut milk,

1 teaspoon curry powder

a pinch of ground ginger

2 teaspoons flour

1. Scale fish, cut off fins and clean thoroughly (see section on preparation of fresh fish). 2. Grind garlic using a rolling pin. 3. Put one tablespoon oil in small bowl or cup. Add in pepper, curry powder, ground garlic, salt ginger, lime juice and mix well. 4. Dart the fish at several places across the skin. 5. Rub the mixture of seasoning onto fish. 6. Put remaining 2 tablespoons of oil in a saucepan. 7. Put saucepan over a lighted charcoal burner. Add seasoned fish. 8. Cover pan with a tight-fitting lid and put charcoal on top (in another container). 9. Leave it to cook for at least 30 minutes, basting at intervals. 10. When fish is cooked, remove from saucepan and keep in serving dish. 11. Peel and slice onion thinly. 12. Blanch tomatoes in boiling water and skin, chop finely. 13. Re-warm remaining fat in the saucepan on charcoal burner. 14. Add in onions, fry until tender. 15. Add in tomatoes, lemon juice and a little salt. Cook covered until quite soft. 16. Add coconut milk into cooking tomatoes and bring to boil, stirring so that coconut milk does not curdle. Add flour already made into a paste. 17. Leave mixture to simmer for 5-10 minutes. 18. Pour it over roasted fish. 19. Serve with *ugali*, rice and vegetables.

NOTE: Alternatively, the fish can be served separately.

BAKED FISH WITH EGGS

3 eggs

2 tablespoons fresh milk

4 thin slices of bread

1/8 teaspoon white pepper

2 pieces of fresh fish (*nguru*)

2 teaspoons lemon juice

1 clove garlic, chopped or ground

1 oz (30 gm) margarine or butter

salt to taste

½ oz (15 gm) oil

Oven temperature:

R 6 (45° F – 23° C)

Wash and cut fish into slices of ¼ inches thick. 2. Heat oven. 3. Grease baking tin well. 4. Mix ground garlic, pepper salt, lemon juice and oil. 5. Rub masala mixture on slices of fish, using a glazing brush or small spoon. 6. Arrange slices in baking tin and put in oven to bake for approximately 20 minutes. 7. Turn from one side to another to get both sides cooked. 8. When cooked keep in a warm place. 9. Break eggs into a bowl one at a time. 10. Add in a little salt, white pepper and milk. 11. Warm small amount of margarine or butter in frying pan. 12. Pour in 1/3 of egg mixture to fry until it is set underneath but creamy on top. 13. Put two slices of fish across the middle and fold omelette over it. Turn carefully to finish cooking. 14. Do the same with remaining 2/3 of the egg mixture and remaining slices of fish. 15. Serve with buttered toast and tomatoes slices.

FISH PASTIES (FISH WITH SHORT PASTRY)

(Makes 4 rounds of filling)

1 glove garlic

8 oz (¼ kg) flour

1 small onion

4 oz (1/8 kg) fat

1 tablespoon oil

1 lime

½ teaspoon salt

1 teaspoon curry powder

3-4 tablespoons water

½ teaspoon pepper

8 oz (¼ kg) flaked fish

¼ teaspoon mustard seeds (optional)

1 pinch ginger

salt to taste

2 medium-sized potatoes

Oven temperature:

R 6 (45° F – 23° C)

1. Prepare and wash fish. 2. Boil fish in small amount of water until cooked. 3. Peel, dice and wash potatoes, and put to boil. 4. Drain stock from the fish. 5. Flake fish, making sure all bones are removed. 6. Mash potatoes well. 7. Peel and chop onion and garlic finely. 8. Heat fat in a saucepan, fry mustard seeds, onion and garlic until tender. 9. Mix mashed potatoes with flaked fish and fried onion mixture. 10. Add pepper, curry powder, ginger, salt and lime juice. Mix well; making sure seasoning is distributed well in the mixture. 11. Put the mixture to stand for a while and heat oven. 12. Make pastry: Sieve flour and salt together. Rub in fat with fingertips. Mix with a little water to make into stiff dough. Divide dough into 4 portions. 13. Make each dough portion into a ball and roll out into rounds of 7 inches diameter and ¼ inches thick. Divide filling into 4 portions. Pile each portion on a round, leaving even ½ inches margin from edge of each round of pastry. 14. Fold pastry over and damp edges with small amount of water. 15. Press edges firmly together, knocking the edge at intervals using fingers. 16. Grease baking sheet and dust with a little flour. 17. Put pastries on baking sheet. 18. Glaze tops with beaten egg or milk using a brush. (Avoid dropping any liquid on the baking sheet). 19. Bake for 35 minutes until light brown. 20. Serve with green vegetables and onion sauce.

DRIED PAPA IN GROUNDNUT MILK

8 oz (¼ kg) piece of dried papa

½ teaspoon chilli powder

1 level tablespoon tomato paste or 1 tomato

2 cloves garlic

1 medium onion

1 ½ teaspoon lime juice

1 dessert spoon oil

1 piece of clove, (optional)

4 oz (120 g) groundnuts, ground

1 pinch of ginger, ground

½ pt (½ litre) water

1 teaspoon curry powder

1.Wash and scrub fish thoroughly to remove sand, put in saucepan. Add water enough to cover. 2. Boil fish for 10 minutes and then wash the skin thoroughly to remove excess salt. Scrub skin if necessary. 3. Peel and slice onion and garlic. 4. Warm fat in a saucepan, add in onion and garlic. Fry until light brown. 5. Add the papa and fry for a while. 6. Add in tomato paste and lime juice and fry. 7. Mix groundnuts with ½ pint (¼ litre) warm water. 8. Add into saucepan, bring mixture to boil and simmer covered until groundnuts are cooked. 9. Serve with ugali or rice and green vegetables.

96

FISH WITH PUMPKIN

1 lb (½ kg) or 1 medium fresh fish

1 teaspoon turmeric

1 lb (½ kg) peeled young pumpkin

1 oz (30 gm) ghee or 1 tablespoon oil

1 cup coconut milk

2 tomatoes

1 large onion

½ lemon

salt and pepper to taste.

1.Cut through centre of pumpkin, remove seeds, peel pumpkin. 2. Cut pumpkin into cubes and keep in cold salty water. 3. Make coconut milk. 4. Boil coconut milk, add some salt and pumpkin cubes, cook for about 10 minutes or until done. 5. Peel onion and slice. 6. Blanch tomatoes in hot water, skin and slice. 7. Prepare fish by removing scales and the insides and wash well in cold water. 8. Heat fat, fry onion, tomatoes and seasonings for a few minutes. 9. Add in the fish. Add some water to make a sauce so that the food will not dry up. 10. Cook fish for about 10-15 minutes, making sure it does not break. 11. Serve cooked pumpkin in a dish, with the fish and sauce poured on the top. 12. Serve hot with rice or *ugali*.

FISH WITH MASALA (SAMAKI WA KUBANIKA)

1 lb (about ½ kg) fresh fish (*changu*)

Masala

4 cloves garlic, chopped

½ teaspoon cardamom seeds, crushed

1 teaspoon turmeric

1 salt teaspoon curry powder

2 green chillies, chopped juice of 1 lime or ½ lemon

1 tablespoon oil.

1. Prepare charcoal stove. 2. Clean fish by removing scales and entrails, wash well in cold water. 3. Prepare the masala and mix into a paste with oil and lime or lemon juice. 4. Dart the fish slightly along both sides at several places. 5. Usually fatty fish is used, but if using white fish, rub with oil first so that the fish will not be too dry. 6. Rub the fish with the masala properly on both sides. 7. When charcoal is hot, put fish over the grilling wire or stick fish through a skewer or grilling sticks. 8. Grill fish for about 15 minutes turning round frequently until cooked. 9. Serve hot or cold with *ugali*, rice and vegetables.

NOTE: You can use an over-grill instead of a charcoal stove.

FISH CUBES

8 oz (½ kg) steak of fresh king-fish

1 egg

¼ pt (1/8 litre) milk and egg or water and egg

2 rounded tablespoons flour

1 level teaspoon salt

1 rounded teaspoon curry powder

½ level teaspoon turmeric

oil for deep frying

1. Wash fish steak and cut into even-size pieces. 2. Sieve dry ingredients together. 3. Beat the egg in a basin, add water. 4. Make a well at the centre of the seasoned flour in a basin. 5. Pour in the egg mixture. 6. Mix well with a wooden spoon into a smooth batter. 7. Taste for seasoning and leave to cool. 8. Heat oil for deep-frying. 9. When oil is hot, dip each piece of fish into the batter mixture and deep-fry until golden brown. 10. Drain off some of the oil on an absorbent piece of paper. 11. Serve hot as a snack for supper or lunch.

NOTE: The size of the fish must be small enough to cook through during frying.

SMOKED FISH IN COCONUT MILK

1 medium smoked fish (*perege*)

1 large onion

¾ pt (3/8 litre) coconut milk

1 large tomato

1 clove garlic

¼ teaspoon chilli powder

salt to taste

1. Soak fish in hot water for 15 minutes. 2. Peel and chop onion, garlic and tomato. 3. Melt fat and fry onion and garlic. Add tomato and fry until they are soft. Add in the rest of seasoning. 4. Put in ½ pint coconut milk. **NOTE:** The coconut milk added here must be from the second squeezing. Leave the first thick milk to be added later on. 5. Wash fish thoroughly and put in the cooking sauce. 6. Simmer gently, until the fish is almost cooked. Then add the ¼ pt. thick coconut milk. Cook for another seven minutes. 7. Serve hot with ugali, rice, bananas or any other carbohydrate, plus a vegetable.

DAGAA AND COCONUT SPINACH

4 oz (120 g) dried *dagaa*

1 medium onion, chopped

1 clove garlic, crushed

1 teaspoon curry powder

2 bunches spinach

2 level teaspoons salt

1 tablespoon (30 gm) fat

¾ pt (3/8 litre) coconut milk

1 tomato, peeled and chopped

1. Remove the heads and wash the *dagaa* thoroughly with hot water. 2. Prepare onions, tomato and garlic, put aside. 3. Melt fat in a saucepan. 4. Fry onions and garlic until soft. 5. Mix curry powder with chopped tomatoes and salt. Add onions and cook covered for a few minutes until tomatoes are soft. 6. Add in the *dagaa*. 7. Add a little water and let mixture boil for 20 minutes.

8. Meanwhile prepare the spinach: put water to boil in a saucepan remove bad leaves from the bunch. Wash the spinach under running water either from the tap or by pouring it from a basin. Blanch the spinach in a saucepan of hot water. Put spinach on

a board and chop with a sharp knife. 9. Add spinach to the cooking *dagaa*. Add curry powder and coconut milk. 10. When mixture starts boiling, leave to simmer for five to ten minutes. Serve hot as a side dish of rice, potatoes and other starchy dishes.

STEWED FISH

1 lb (½ kg) fish

1 onion

1 large tomato

juice of ½ lemon

1 tablespoon ghee

salt to taste

1 cup water

1 teaspoon flour

1. Prepare and clean fish and dart in several places. 2. Slice onions and tomatoes. 3. Mix salt with lemon juice and rub on both sides of the fish. 4. Fry onions and tomatoes in fat with lid on, until onions are tender. 5. Mix little water with flour to make a thin paste. Add this to the cooking onions. 6. Add the remaining water, then the fish and gently cook covered until the fish is cooked. Turn carefully if necessary, otherwise baste only. *Do not stir.* 7. When cooked the stew should be thick. 8. Serve hot. Be careful not to break up the fish.

FRESH PRAWN CURRY (KAMBA)

6 oz (180 g) fresh shelled prawns, boiled

1 large onion

3 cloves garlic

1 green chilli

2 teaspoons curry powder

1 teaspoon turmeric

juice of ½ lemon

1 fresh tomato or 2 teaspoons tomato paste

1 potato

3 teaspoons ghee

salt to taste

1 teaspoon *kotimiri*, chopped

1. Prepare prawns. 2. Peel and chop garlic and onion. 3. Chop the chilli. 4. Prepare coconut milk. 5. Skin and chop tomato if used. Dice potatoes. 6. Mix curry powder, chilli, salt, turmeric, lemon juice and chopped herbs. 7. Heat fat in a frying pan. Add onion and garlic and fry for a few minutes. 8. Add mixed spices, then tomato or tomato paste. 9. After a few minutes add prawns, potatoes and coconut milk. 10. Cook gently until the prawns are cooked and the sauce is very thick. 11. Taste for salt and serve hot.

FISH CURRY

8 oz (240 gm) fish steak

1 large tomato

1 onion

2 cloves garlic

1 teaspoon curry powder

a pinch of chilli powder or 1 whole chilli

2 teaspoons grate coconut

2 teaspoons lemon juice

1 cup water

salt to taste

6 tablespoons milk

2 tablespoons oil or 1 tablespoon ghee

1. Wash and cut fish into cubes. 2. Peel and chop both onion and garlic. 3. Skin tomato and chop. 4. Mix the chilli, coconut, lemon juice, salt, curry powder. 5. Heat fat in a frying pan. 6. Fry the onions and garlic. Add the mixed spices. 7. Fry for a few minutes, then add tomatoes and let them cook for a while. 8. Add the fish, then milk and water. 9. Cook gently for 15-20 minutes or until the fish is cooked, depending on the size of the fish cubes. 10. When ready serve hot.

FRIED WHOLE FISH

2 whole medium fish

Masala

1 teaspoon turmeric

1 tablespoon oil or ghee

½ tablespoon lemon juice

salt to taste

chilli to taste, *if desired*

fat for shallow frying

1. Prepare and clean fish if fresh. If frozen, thaw it well and wipe dry with clean cloth. 2. Dart the fish several places on both sides. 3. Mix oil, turmeric, lemon juice, chilli and salt. 4. Rub the fish with the masala on both sides and leave to stand for 10-15 minutes. 5. Heat fat till hot. 6. Quickly fry each fish on sides, then lower heat and fry gently until cooked, and golden brown on the outside. 7. Use as required, either for preparing a fish dish or serving whole on its own as part of a meal.

NOTE: If fish is fried in hot fat through out it becomes hard and tough as well as over browned.

SAUSAGE BATTER BAKE

(Makes 18-20 rounds)

½ lb (¼ kg) pork or beef sausages

1 onion, finely chopped pinch of pepper

1 teaspoon curry powder

Batter

4 oz (120 g) flour

1 egg

¼ pint (1/8 litre) milk and egg or water and egg

½ level teaspoon salt

Oven temperature

R 4 (350 º F-175 º C) then R 6 (900 º F – 200 º C)

1. Make the batter mixture and leave to cool. Sift flour and salt into a bowl. Beat the egg into a small basin. Make a well at the centre of the flour; pour in the beaten egg and the liquid. Mix with a wooden spoon avoiding any lumps. Leave to cool well covered for about 15 minutes. 2. Soak the sausage meat in cold water for 5 minutes to loosen the skin. 3. Slit the sausage along its length, remove the meat, mix it with the chopped onion, pepper and curry powder for more flavour on a floured board. 4. Divide the mixture into the small rounds. 5. Grease two baking patty tins. 6. Fill the tins with the sausage rounds and flatten them slightly. 7. Bake the sausage first in moderate oven for 30 minutes. 8. Remove the meat rounds from the baking tins, fill each hole with the batter mixture (2 dessertspoons in each). 9. Return the meat rounds into the tins on top of the batter mixture. 10. Increase heat, bake again for about 15 minutes until the batter is set and cooked. 11. Serve hot or cold as a snack.

BEEF, PORK AND BANANA ROAST

8 oz (kg) lean pork

8 oz (kg) beef steak

4 green bananas (*mshare*)

1 cauliflower

½ lemon

1 medium sized carrot

1 medium sized onion

1 tomato or 1 level tablespoon tomato paste

¼ teaspoon pepper

salt to taste

3 tablespoons oil

1 teaspoon oil

1 teaspoon curry powder

water

1 clove garlic.

Oven temperature

R 6 (450 º F – 230 ºC then R 4 (350 º F – 175 º C)

1. Wash, cut the pork and beef into slices of ¼ inch thickness. 2. Using meat tenderizer or rolling pin, beat the slices of meat and pork to make them tender. 3. Mix curry powder, crushed garlic, salt, lemon juice and 1 tablespoon of oil. 4. Rub the mixture (masala) on to the slices of meat. 5. Put 1 tablespoon of oil in a roasting tin and heat well. 6. Add the pieces of meat and put in pre-heated oven. This can also be done over a charcoal stove. 7. After a few minutes, lower heat. Leave the meat to cook gently, basting from time to time. 8. Meanwhile wash and chop the cauliflower. 9. Put water in a saucepan to boil, add in a little salt. 10. Add in the cauliflower and leave to cook until tender. 11. When the meat is cooked keep it in a warm place. 12. Heat the remaining oil in a saucepan, fry onion and garlic until tender. 13. Blanch, skin, chop the tomato and fry (or add in the tomato puree). 14. Add in the boiled cauliflower, then the cauliflower, then the juices from the roasted meat. 15. Leave to cook for 5 minutes. 16. Peel the bananas and scrape off the outer skin. 17. Put in a baking tin or

shallow pan and roast over a charcoal burner or in the oven. 18. Keep turning them until they are dry and well cooked. 19. Arrange the slices of meat in the idle of a serving dish. 20. Arrange the bananas on the edge and pour the cauliflower mixture on top of the meat. 21. Garnish with chopped green herbs or sliced fresh tomatoes. **NOTE:** Alternatively, the meat can be roasted on open fire for *mishikaki*, and bananas likewise. Then the bananas are sliced in the middle, lengthwise and buttered. The bananas and meat are served dry, i.e. without the cauliflower mixture or with the cauliflower mixture served in a separated dish.

CURRIED TONGUE

6-8 oz (180-240 g) tongue, boiled and sliced

1 onion, chopped

½ green chilli, chopped

2 cloves of garlic, crushed

1 teaspoon turmeric or curry powder

1 tomato, chopped or 1 tablespoon tomato paste

1 tablespoon oil or ghee

¼ cup water

salt to taste

1 bunch *kotimiri*, chopped

1. Heat the fat in a saucepan and fry the onions, garlic and chilli. 2. Add the seasoning, then the tomato and fry for a few minutes. 3. Add the tongue, then the water. Stir well. 4. Taste for salt and continue to cook over low heat for 10 minutes. 5. Serve hot.

5
LENTILS, BEANS, PEAS AND NUTS

BEAN SAUCE

4 oz (120 g) dried beans

1 onion , chopped

2 oz (60 g) fat

1 pt (½litres) water

1 oz (30 g) flour

¼ pt (1/8litres) milk or coconut milk

salt to taste

1. Soak beans overnight, take off skins. 2. Heat fat and fry onions until tender but not brown. 3. Add beans, water and salt. Boil for 2 or 3 hours, or until beans are soft. 4. Stir milk or coconut milk into flour. Add to bean sauce and boil for ten minutes. 5. Serve hot with any starchy dish.

NOTE: Cooking time depends on type of beans. Beans should not be mushy.

BEANS AND VEGETABLE AU GRATIN

6 oz (180 g) fresh beans (french beans)

4 oz (120 g) green maize off the cob

1 large firm tomato

1 medium carrot

Salt to taste

Cheese sauce

½ pt (¼litre) milk and vegetable stock or water

1 level tablespoon margarine

1 rounded tablespoon flour

¾ cup vegetables stock or water

2 oz (60 g) grated cheese

salt and white pepper to taste

1. Wash and cut fresh beans into slices. 2. Scrape and shred carrot into thin strips. 3. Wash maize kernels. 4. Steam or cook maize kernels, carrot and fresh beans in little boiling water with a bit of salt till tender, or cook each separately. 5. When cooked, drain and put vegetables in a heatproof dish or casserole. If vegetables were cooked separately, arrange them in the dish in alternate layers. 6. Wash and cut tomato into rings and arrange them on top of the vegetables. 7. Prepare cheese sauce. Put flour and fat in a saucepan and then heat it stirring with a wooden spoon until flour has flour has absorbed all fat but not browned. Add milk gradually, stirring constantly to avoid forming lumps, until it thickens. Add seasonings vegetables stock and grated cheese leaving some of it for sprinkling on top. Stir carefully until all cheese melts. 8. Pour sauce over vegetables. 9. Sprinkle remaining grated cheese on top of the sauce

and put under grill or in a moderately hot oven tillthe top is slightly brown. 10. Serve hot in the same dish.

GREEN SPLIT BEAN CURRY

1 cup split beans

1 onion, finely chopped

A piece of ginger, chopped

½ green chilli

2-3 cloves garlic

1 teaspoon coriander seeds

2 teaspoons turmeric

salt to taste

1 pt (½litres) thick coconut milk

1. Wash and soak beans. 2. Make ½ litre (1pt) thin coconut milk from leftover coconut (*machicha*). 3. Grind coriander seeds, garlic, ginger, chilli and mix with salt and turmeric. 4. Boil beans in thin coconut milk until soft and liquid almost dried. 5. Add ground spices, onion and thick coconut milk to the cooking beans. Continue to cook till curry becomes thick but not dry 20-30 minutes. 6. Serve hot with rice or *ugali*.

"KIBURU" BANANA WITH BEANS (BROWN BEANS)

12 oz (360 g) dry beans

4 green bananas soft type (*matoke*)

2 cups water or bone stock (optional)

1 tablespoon ghee or butter

1 medium onion, finely chopped

salt to taste

1. Wash beans thoroughly and put to boil until nearly ready; (by this time very little liquid should remain). 2. Peel the bananas, scrape very thinly, cut into neat pieces, then put in boiling water for a few minutes to wash out the sticky sap. Drain. 3. Take the onions, bananas and ghee and add to the cooking beans. Add salt to taste. 4. Add stock and continue to cook till both bananas and beans are cooked. 5. Mash carefully, preferably with a three prong local wooden masher. 6. Add more stock or water if necessary until the mixture is a thick pouring consistency. Serve hot or cold.

NOTE: One expects to find whole beans in this mixture. This dish is traditionally done in a clay pot, but a heavy saucepan is equally satisfactory.

SHIRO BANANA WITH BEANS

12 oz (360 g) dry beans (*maharage*)

4 green bananas (soft type or *matoke*)

1 cup bone stock or water

1 tablespoon ghee or other fat

1 medium onion, finely chopped

Salt to taste

1. Follow same method as for "*Kiburu*" but leave mixture stiff like mashed potatoes or even stiffer. 2. Serve with vegetable whenever possible. *Traditionally this dish is popular as a packed meal for farmers.*

BEAN PASTIES

8 oz (¼ kg) beans

8 oz (¼ kg) flour

4 oz (120 g) cooking oil

2 eggs

4 pt (1/8 litre) water

1 onion

1 tomato

1 teaspoon curry powder

2 teaspoons salt

Oven temperature

R 6 (400ºF – 200ºC)

1. Wash and boil beans in salted water. 2. While beans are boiling, make a short crust pastry. Rub fat into flour. Add in ¼ pt (1/8 litre) water. Using a pastry knife mixing into a soft dough, but not sticky. Set dough in a cool place. 3. Chop onions and tomatoes. 4. Drain water from beans, mash beans finely. 5. Fry onion and the tomato. 6. Add in curry powder. 7. Add in mashed beans and fry them for 6 minutes. 8. Remove from heat, cool and add beaten eggs. 9. Roll out pastry and cut into 8 rounds. 10. One each round put two tablespoons of fried beans. 11. Wet the edges of the pastry, enclose filling. Seal edges with a knife. 12. Glaze the top with milk or egg. 13. Make a hole at the centre to let steam out. 14. Bake for 30 minutes. 15. Can be served for snack or a packed meal.

SOYA BEAN SCONES

4 oz (120 g) bean

4 oz (120 g) flour

2 oz (60 g) margarine

2 teaspoons baking powder

1 egg

a pinch of salt

¼ pt (1/8 litre) fresh milk

1. Wash and soak beans overnight. 2. Drain water and skin. 3. Boil beans in salt water until soft. 4. Mince them finely or mash them. 5. Rub fat in flour, and in minced beans. 6. Using a pastry knife, mix flour and beans well, then add in beaten egg and

milk, making a dough which is soft but not sticky. 7. Roll into a big round about ½ inch (1.2 cm) and starting from the centre, cut into 8 triangles. Glaze these with milk. 8. Bake in a hot oven R 6 for 20 minutes (450 ºF – 225 ºC). Serve hot with butter for breakfast. They can also be used as packed meal.

CHOROKO BAJIA

8 oz (¼ kg) *choroko*

1 teaspoon chilli powder

1 teaspoon curry powder

2 eggs

1 clove garlic

fat for deep frying

salt to taste

1. Wash and soak *choroko* overnight. Cook until tender, drain. 2. Mince them or pound. 3. Into a mixing bowl, add in all spices chopped garlic and salt. 4. Beat eggs and add them into mixture to bind. 5. Put fat into a saucepan. 6. Shape mixture into small balls and deep fry them till brown outside and cooked inside. 7. Serve with stew, or with green vegetables.

NOTE: A good item for packed meal.

DENGU BAJIA

4 oz (120 gm) *dengu* flour

2 oz (60 gm) peeled potatoes

¼ pt (1/8 lt) milk

½ whole green chilli

2 cloves garlic

1 level teaspoon salt

1. Peel and slice potatoes into very thin slices. 2. Crush garlic and chilli. 3. Mix chili with *dengu* flour and potatoes. 4. Make whole mixture into a thick paste with ¼ pt milk. 5. Drop by tablespoonful in deep fat, fry till golden brown and potatoes are cooked. Serve as a snack.

SWEET POTATO BAJIA

8 oz (240 gm) *dengu* flour

4 oz (120 gm) sweet potatoes

1 green chilli, crushed

3 cloves garlic, crushed

1 level teaspoon salt

½ pt (¼lt) milk or water

1. Wash, peel and slice potatoes very thinly. 2. Mix *dengu* flour with raw potatoes, onion, garlic and chilli. 3. Add liquid into flour and make a smooth paste. 4. Fry the mixture by spoonful in deep fat fry two minutes or until golden brown. Serve hot for snacks.

BEAN FRITTERS

2 oz (60 gm) dried beans

1 onion, chopped

1 dessert spoon wheat flour

¼ pt (1/8lt) milk

fat for shallow frying

1. Soak beans overnight, remove skins. 2. Cook beans until soft, then mash a little. 3. Fry onions in hot fat until tender. Prepare flour paste by mixing flour with milk to a smooth paste. Mix together beans, flour paste, onion and salt. Heat fat. Spoon in the mixture, by spoonfuls. Fry each side until brown. Fat should cover the bottom of the pan – add more if needed while frying.

COCONUT BEANS (BOROHOA)

8 oz (¼ kg) beans

2 onions

2 oz fat

½ teaspoon turmeric powder

1 oz (30 g) flour

½ pt (¼ litre) coconut milk or cow's milk

salt and pepper to taste

1 pt (½ litre) stock

1. Wash and soak beans overnight, then skin them. 2. Chop onions, heat fat and fry onions until tender but not brown. 3. Add turmeric powder, then beans, salt and stock. Leave to cook until soft. 4. Stir milk or coconut milk into flour, add to beans and leve to simmer for about 10 minutes. 5. Serve hot with any starchy dish.

MASHED POTATOES WITH BEANS (VIAZI VYA KUPONDA NA MAHARAGE)

8 oz (¼ kg) sweet potatoes

3 oz (90 g) beans

1 onion

1 tablespoon fat

1 teaspoon turmeric powder

salt and pepper to taste

1. Sort out and wash beans. Boil until soft. 2. Peel potatoes and cut into small cubes. 3. Prepare onions, fry them. Add potatoes, turmeric powder, salt and pepper. Add stock or water and leave to cook. 4. When almost soft add cooked beans. Simmer for 10 minutes. 5. Mash the mixture till soft. Serve with any stew or vegetables.

COCONUT BOROHOA

4 oz (120 g) rod beans

1 medium tomato

1 medium onion

¼ teaspoon turmeric powder

1 teaspoon curry powder

¼ pt (1/8 litre) coconut milk

1 level tablespoon fat

¼ level teaspoon ground black pepper

1. Soak beans overnight, peel off outer skins. 2. Boil beans with some salt till they are soft. Very little liquid should be left. 3. Peel and chop onion, garlic, and tomato. 4. Fry onions and garlic till tender. Add tomatoes, curry powder, turmeric, pepper and salt. 5. Stir in beans, fry for about 5 minutes, then add coconut milk. 6. Lower heat; simmer gently until coconut milk is cooked. Serve hot with rice or *ugali*.

KISHUMBA (SWEET POTATOES WITH BEANS)

4 oz (120 g) beans

16 oz (½ kg) sweet potatoes

¼ teaspoon bicarbonate of soda

1 level teaspoon salt

1 tablespoon butter

1. Wash and soak beans overnight. 2. Boil them in salt water. 3. Peel and wash potatoes. 4. Add bicarbonate of soda to beans. 5. Cook potatoes separately. 6. Remove from heat, add butter mash well. 7. When potatoes are smooth, mix with cooked beans. If mixture is too stiff, fresh milk can be used to dilute it to desired consistency. 8. Serve with vegetables, e.g. spinach.

MILK KIBURU II (BEANS WITH BANANA)

8 oz (¼ kg) beans

½ pt (¼ litre) fresh milk

1 oz (30 g) fat

salt to taste

6 green bananas

a pinch bicarbonate of soda

1. Wash beans and boil in salt water. 2. Peel bananas and slice thinly. 3. Wash bananas and add into boiling beans. 4. Reduce heat and simmer gently till beans are cooked. 5. Add in bicarbonate of soda, continue cooking beans. 6. Add in salt, fat and stock on water. 7. When all is cooked, mash bananas well, and dilute with fresh milk. 8. Stir in beans and serve hot for lunch or supper.

BEAN CROQUETTES

8 oz (¼ kg) beans

3 eggs

1 level teaspoon salt

1 level teaspoon curry powder

fat for deep frying

1 onion, chopped

breadcrumbs

1. Wash and soak beans overnight. 2. Drain water and skin. 3. Boil beans in salt water till soft but not mushy. 4. Drain water completely and mash beans. 5. Add in egg yolks, then curry powder, salt and onion. 6. Using a pastry knife, mix to a stiff consistency. 7. Shape mixture into crescents or bean-shape. 8. Dip bean mixture into egg whites, then roll breadcrumbs in portions. 9. Fry in hot fat until brown in colour. Serve with some vegetables for a snack, or use for a packed meal.

MASHED POTATOES AND BEANS

1 lb (½ kg) potatoes

3 oz (90 g) dried beans

1 level teaspoon salt

1 oz (30 g) butter or margarine

1. Soak beans overnight. 2. Boil them in hot water. 3. Peel potatoes and cut into small cubes. 4. When beans are almost cooked, add potatoes. Add salt. 5. Cover saucepan tightly and cook over a moderate heat, till both potatoes and beans are soft. 6. Mash the potatoes at the lep until soft. Then mix them well with beans. Add melted butter or margarine and mix well 7. Serve hot with a vegetable.

GROUNDNUT AND BEAN UGALI

1lb (½ kg) beans

1 cup groundnuts, ground

1 large onion

1 cup maize flour

salt to taste

water to cook

1. Wash and soak beans overnight. Skin them. 2. Boil beans until cooked. 3. Slice onion and fry lightly for a few minutes. 4. Mix flour and groundnuts with a little water to make a paste. Add this paste to frying onion. 5. Add water, a little at a time, stirring all the time until a thick porridge is formed. 6. Mash beans thoroughly and add to cooking mixture, stir with a wooden spoon. Add more flour if necessary and continue to cook for another 15 minutes. 7. When ready, ugali should be like a soft maize ugali in consistency. 8. Serve hot with vegetables.

MSETO (RICE LENTILS)

6 oz (180 g) rice

3 oz (90 g) lentils (*dengu*)

1 medium onion, chopped

1 oz (30 g) fat

1 teaspoon tomato paste (optional)

½ teaspoon salt

1.Wash rice and soak in water. 2. Wash lentils and boil them in enough salted water until just soft. 3. Heat fat ad fry onions until soft. Add in tomato paste and fry. Add in lentils and fry. 4. Drain rice and fry together with lentils for two minutes. Taste for salt. 5. Add in coconut milk and bring to boil, then simmer until rice and *choroko* are cooked but dry. 6. Serve hot with a stew, vegetables and other accompaniments.

CHOROKO PILAU

4 oz (120 g) shelled *choroko* (green dhal)

6 oz (180 g) rice

2 medium-sized potatoes

1 medium onion

1 teaspoon salt

½ teaspoon curry powder

4 cloves

2 cardamom seeds

1 cup coconut milk

1 tablespoon fat

1. Wash *choroko*, cook in boiling salted water until almost done. Cooking time depends on dryness of the *choroko*. 2. Wash and leave rice to soak. 3. Peel potatoes and cut into dices. 4. Slice and chop onions. 5. Melt fat in a pan, fry onions, but do

not brown them. 6. Add rice and fry for a few minutes. Add cloves, cardamom seeds, curry powder and salt to taste. 7. Add cooked *choroko*, potatoes and coconut milk. Stir well. Cover and leave to simmer slowly. 8. Stir occasionally adding more liquid if necessary until all ingredients are cooked. 9. Put pan in moderate oven to dry uncovered or covered with a lid upon which burning charcoal is placed. 10. When ready serve with a sauce (*mchuzi*) and vegetables.

CURRIED CHOROKO

8 oz (240 g) *choroko*

2 medium onions

1 teaspoon curry powder

2 medium tomatoes

Salt to taste

2 cloves garlic

2 tablespoons palm oil or other oil

1. Boil *choroko* in salt water until cooked. 2. Meanwhile peel and slice onions, tomatoes and garlic. 3. Put palm oil, onions, tomatoes, curry powder and salt in a pan. Fry lightly for a few minutes. Cover pan and continue to simmer until mixture is soft and cooked. 4. Add cooked *choroko*, continue to cook for another 10-15 minutes, allowing beans to absorb flavour and spice. Serve hot.

NOTE: The curry tastes better, if little or no water is left after boiling the *choroko*, therefore avoid using *choroko* stock in curry.

MBAAZI ROJO

8 oz (240 gm) shelled *mbaazi*

1 onion

1 tablespoon oil

salt to taste

Sauce

2 large tomatoes ½ tablespoon tomato paste (optional)

1 *bringal*

1 green chilli

2 onions

4 cloves garlic

1 lime or lemon

½ teaspoon curry powder

1 tablespoon ghee or oil

16 oz (½ kg) potatoes

salt to taste

1. Wash *mbaazi* and put to boil in salt water. 2. Chop onion and add to cooking *mbaazi*, continue to cook until soft. Drain any surplus water. 3. Blanch tomatoes, skin and chop. 4. Chop onions and garlic. 5. Peel potatoes and *bringals*. Slice as for chips. 6. Heat fat in a pan, add onions, *bringals*, tomatoes, lemon juice, seasonings and cook for 5-10 minutes. Add potatoes; cook till all vegetables are done. 7. Serve *mbaazi* either in a dish with sauce poured on top, or serve on a large plate arranged decoratively.

SAVOURY BEAN BALLS

4 oz (120 g) lentils (*dengu*)

1 teaspoon salt

2 large onions, chopped

1 teaspoon turmeric

1 green chilli, chopped

1 egg, beaten

½ oz (15 g) fat for frying

½ tablespoon flour

1. Clean lentils. Put them in 1 pt. salted water, boil until soft. Make sure water is completely dried up. 2. Mash lentils. 3. Fry onions and chilli until just soft. 4. Mix fried onions with a little beaten egg and mashed lentils. 5. Divide mixture into balls. 6. Roll balls lightly into flour and then in beaten egg. 7. Fry the balls in deep fat until golden brown.

PEAS AND GROUNDNUT SAUCE

4 oz (120 g) shelled peas

3 oz (90 g) green maize, off the cob

1 onion

1 large fresh tomato

½ teaspoon curry powder

¾ cup groundnuts

1 tablespoon cooking oil
salt to taste

1. Wash both maize and peas. 2. Boil the green maize for about 10 minutes and then add peas. Cook them both till soft. 3. Skin and slice tomato. 4. Skin and chop onion. 5. Heat oil in a pan and fry the onion until golden brown. 6. Add tomato, curry powder, salt and fry for a while. 7. Mix groundnuts with stock from maize and peas. 8. Add in the boiled peas and maize. Stir well. Add groundnuts then lower the heat and simmer for 20-25 minutes (if the mixture is too thick add more water). 9. Serve hot with *ugali* or rice, or other starchy dish.

SORGHUM WITH COWPEAS (MCHANYATO WA MTAMA NA KUNDE)

1 small onion

1 oz (30 g) fat or margarine

salt and pepper to taste

4 oz (120 g) sorghum millet

3 oz (85 to 90 g) fresh cowpeas (*kunde*)

1. Wash sorghum and put to boil. 2. Peel *kunde* (if fresh), wash. 3. When sorghum is half-cooked, add *kunde* and salt. Continue cooking. 4. chop onions add to the sorghum and *kunde*. 5. When sorghum and *kunde* are soft, add fat and pepper, and stir well. Leave to cook slowly till completely dry like cooked rice. 6. Serve with vegetables.

RICE MSETO

4 oz (120 g) rice

2 oz (60 g) *choroko*

1 onion, chopped

1 tomato, chopped

¼ teaspoon curry powder

¼ teaspoon turmeric

salt and pepper to taste

1 tablespoon fat

½ pt (¼litre) coconut milk

1. Clean and wash *choroko*. Boil until nearly cooked. 2 Prepare coconut milk. 3. Clean and wash rice. Boil until nearly cooked. 4. Prepare tomato and onion. 5. Fry onion in fat. Add tomato and spices. 6. Add *choroko* to the mixture, then rice and coconut milk. Stir occasionally. 7. Cook with gentle heat until ready. Serve with a vegetable or another accompaniment.

COCONUT KUNDE

4 oz (120 g) *kunde*

1 clove garlic

1 onion, chopped

1 tomato, chopped

¼ pt (1/8litre) coconut milk

½ teaspoon curry powder or turmeric

1 tablespoon fat

salt to taste

1. Clean and wash *kunde*, boil until nearly cooked. 2. Prepare ¼ pt coconut milk. 3. Heat fat in a pan and fry on ions. 4. Add tomatoes and spices. 5. Drain *kunde*. 6. Add *kunde* and then coconut milk. Stir occasionally. 7. Cook gently for about 15 – 20 minutes. 8. Serve with a starchy dish, e.g. rice or ugali, and a vegetable.

COCONUT MBAAZI

4 oz (120 g) fresh shelled *mbaazi*

1 onion, chopped

1 tomato, chopped

salt to taste

½ green chilli, chopped

1 tablespoon fat

¼ teaspoon turmeric powder

½ teaspoon curry powder

½ pt (¼litre) coconut milk

1. Wash *mbaazi*, boil until soft. 2. Prepare thick coconut milk. 3. Prepare onion, chilli and tomatoes. 4. Heat fat in a pan and fry the onions. Add chilli, tomatoes and other seasonings. 5. Strain *mbaazi,* add to tomato and onion mixture. 6. Add coconut milk, cook for about 7-10 minutes. 7. Serve with a starchy dish, e.g. rice or ugali.

SWEET POTATOES AND KUNDE (COWPEAS)

4 oz (120 g) *kunde*

6 medium sweet potatoes

1 fresh chilli, chopped

salt to taste

1 tablespoon fat

1 onion, chopped

1 tomato, chopped

3 teaspoons turmeric

2 pt (1/8litre) coconut milk, (optional)

1. Soak *kunde* overnight. Boil until soft. 2. Prepare coconut milk. 3. Peel, wash and slice potatoes, boil until nearly cooked. 4. Prepare onions, chilli and tomatoes. 5. Heat fat in a pan and fry onion and chill until slightly brown, add tomato and spices. 6. Add *kunde*, then coconut milk. Continue cooking, stiring occasionally. 7. Drain potatoes and add to the mixture, simmer for about 10-15 minutes. 8. Serve hot as a main dish with a vegetable.

KANDE WITH PEAS

4 oz (120 g) pounded maize

3 oz (90 gm) dry peas

1 onion, chopped

1 large tomato

½ pt (¼litre) coconut milk

2 cloves garlic, crushed

½ chilli, cut into rings

1 level teaspoon turmeric

1 dessertspoon tomato paste

salt to taste

1 tablespoon oil

1. Wash maize and peas and soak for several hours. 2. Boil maize in salty water until half cooked, add peas. 3. Fry onions until golden brown, add tomatoes, then tomato paste and seasonings. 4. Add in maize and peas and stir for a while. 5. Add in coconut milk and simmer for 5 minutes more. 6. Serve hot with vegetables, meat or fish.

GREEN DHAL AND SORGHUM

4 oz (120 g) millet

3 oz (90 g) dhal (*choroko*)

1 medium onion, chopped

1 level teaspoon salt

1 dessertspoon fat

¼ teaspoon turmeric

1 pt water

1 teaspoon tomato paste or 1 medium fresh tomato, chopped

1. Wash millet and put in a large saucepan with two pints water to boil for 1¼ hour, till soft. 2. Meanwhile wash *choroko* and put in water to boil for ¾ hour. 3. Heat fat in a saucepan, fry onions over low heat until tender. 4. Mix turmeric with tomato paste and fry with onions. 5. Add in cooked millet and fry together. 6. Add in *choroko*, then more liquid. 7. Add salt and leave mixture for simmer for 20-30 minutes. Serve hot with meat or other protein dish. **NOTE:** This dish can also be served alone.

KUNDE AND BANANA BAKE

2 cups fresh shelled beans (*kunde*)

2 green bananas

1 small onion, finely chopped

salt

1 tablespoon seasoned flour (salt and white pepper)

1 tablespoon cooking oil

1 egg, beaten

a little milk to glaze

Oven temperature

R 6 (400ºF – 200ºC)

1. Wash *kunde*, cook in boiling water with a bit of salt till soft. Drain and mash while hot. 2. Peel and scrape bananas, cut into thin strips. 3. Wash them in hot water and cook till tender. Drain and mash. Sautee onion in a little fat till tender. 4. Mix cooked *kunde*, beaten egg, bananas and onions. Taste for flavour. 5. Preheat oven and grease baking sheet. 6. Put *kunde* and banana mixture on a board dusted with seasoned flour and allow to cool. 7. Shape each piece into roll and cut into six equal pieces. Shape each piece into a flat, round cake. 8. Coat with seasoned flour. Brush with milk. 9. Put on the baking sheet and bake in oven on centre shell for 20-25 minutes. 10. When ready serve hot. Alternatively, the cakes can also be deep-fried or shallow fried and should be drained on absorbent paper before serving. There is no need to glaze the cakes before frying.

GREEN PEAS AND BANANAS

4 green bananas

4 oz (120 g) green peas

salt to taste

1 onion, chopped

1 tomato, chopped

1 tablespoon fat

½ teaspoon curry powder

¼ teaspoon turmeric

¼ pt (1/8litre) coconut milk

1. Shell peas, put to boil until nearly cooked. Let aside. 2. Meanwhile, prepare coconut milk. 3. Peel and slice onions, and tomatoes. 4. Peel, slice and wash bananas. Boil them in slightly salted water until soft. 5. Heat fat in a large pan. Fry onions until light brown. Add tomatoes and spices. 6. Add peas, then coconut milk, stirring occasionally. 7. Drain bananas and add to the mixture. Simmer for about 7-10 minutes.
8. Serve hot as a main dish with leafy vegetables.

CHOROKO, MILLET AND CASHEWNUTS

4 oz (120 g) millet

3 oz (90 g) *choroko*

2 0z (60 g) chashewnuts, ground

1 onion, chopped

2 cloves garlic, crushed

1 tomato, chopped

1 level teaspoon curry powder

1 level teaspoon turmeric

salt to taste

water

1 tablespoon oil

1. Wash both millet and *choroko* separately. 2. Cook separately in boiling water until soft. 3. Fry onions, ad in tomatoes, curry powder, turmeric, garlic, salt and cashew nuts. 4. Add in millet and *choroko* and fry for a while. Add in hot water or stock and simmer until cooked but dry, like cooked rice. 5. Serve hot with vegetables, meat or fish.

GROUNDNUT CUTLETS

 4 oz (120 g) groundnuts

1 onion

1 tomato

small unripe mango

1 tablespoon breadcrumbs

1 egg beaten

3 tablespoons fat

salt and pepper to taste

a little milk

1. Fry, shell and grind the groundnuts in a little fat. Chop onion, mango and tomato. 2. Heat one tablespoon fat in a skillet as heavy saucepan, fry onion, mango and tomato. 3. Add the fried mixture to the groundnuts. 4. Bind the mixture with beaten egg to give it a moist consistency. 5. Shape into cutlets, brush with beaten egg and coat lightly with breadcrumbs. Fry in remaining fat until crisp and brown.

GROUNDNUTS IN RICE

8 oz (240 g) rice

4 oz (120 g) groundnuts

2 cloves garlic, chopped

salt and pepper to taste

1 pt stock

1 onion, chopped

1. Put stock to boil. Add salt, garlic and chopped onion. 2. Prepare rice, wash and soak it. 3. Cook rice till almost soft. 4. Roast groundnuts, shell and finely chop them. 5. Mix rice and groundnuts. Cover pot and cook till soft. 6. Sift the mixture and serve hot with vegetables.

MASANGU (MAIZE WITH GROUNDNUTS)

8 oz (¼ kg) pounded maize

8 oz (¼ kg) groundnuts

1 tablespoon fat

1 tomato

½ pt ((¼litre) coconut milk

salt to taste

1 teaspoon curry powder

1. Wash the pounded maize well. 2. Boil in salty water until done. 3. Fry groundnuts, shell them and finely grind them. 4. Chop onions and tomatoes finely. Add onion, tomatoes and seasoning to cooking maize. 5. Add groundnuts, stir well until all is mixed. Add in coconut milk plus fat and continue cooking for another 10-15 minutes. 6. Serve hot as a main dish with vegetables.

GROUNDNUT PORRIDGE (UJI WA KARANGA)

8 oz (¼ kg) groundnuts

4 oz (120 g) maize flour

2 oz (60 g) sugar

1 oz (30 g) butter or margarine

1 pt (½litre) sour milk

lemon juice

1 pt (½litre) water

1. Fry or roast groundnuts and shell them, then grind finely. 2. Boil water in a saucepan. 3. Stir in maize flour and keep stirring until it thickens without any lumps. 4. Cook for 10 minutes. 5. Add in groundnut flour and cook again for 2 minutes. 6. Add in sugar, lemon juice and lastly milk. Stir well. 7. Serve hot for breakfast, or as a dish for invalids and infants.

GROUNDNUT FLOUR

as many groundnuts as required

Roast groundnuts. 2. Remove outside skins. 3. Pound and sift them to obtain the flour or grind them to a paste.

6
CEREALS, GRAINS, TUBERS AND OTHER STARCHES

UGALI (STIFF PORRIDGE)

8 oz(240g) maize flour

½ pt (¼litre) milk

½ pt (¼litre) water

1oz (30 gm) margarine or fat (optional)

salt (optional)

1. Put water to boil, add fat, if used. 2. Make a paste with milk and some flour.
3. When water has boiled, add in the paste and stir. 4. Add in remaining flour and mix, using a wooden spoon, to a stiff porridge until cooked. When done, *ugali* should leave the sides of the pan. 5. Serve hot with vegetables, meat, fish or beans.

KANDE WITH GROUNDNUTS (MAKANDE YA KARANGA)

8 oz (240 g) pounded maize

4 (120 g) groundnuts

½ oz (15 g) fat

4 oz (120 g) beans

1 onion, chopped

¼ pt (1/8litre) milk

1. Wash pounded maize, put to boil. 2. Wash beans, after about 10 minutes add beans to maize. Leave to cook until soft. 3. Prepare groundnuts by pounding, mix with milk, add salt. 4. Prepare onion, then fry. 5. Add groundnuts. Stir mixture while it boils for about 5 minutes. Add cooked maize and beans. Mix well and leave to cook slowly until ready. 6. Serve either dry or with a small amount of liquid still left.

PLAIN KANDE (MAIZE WITH BEANS)

4 oz (120 g) pounded maize

1 onion, chopped

½ teaspoon curry powder

½ pt (¼litre) coconut milk (optional)

1 tablespoon fat

1 tomato, chopped

½ teaspoon turmeric

salt to taste

1. Soak beans overnight. Soak maize overnight. 3. Boil maize in water until soft. 4. Boil beans in water until soft. 5. Prepare coconut milk. 6. Peel and slice onions, tomatoes. 7. Heat fat in a pan and fry onions until light brown. Add tomatoes and spices. 8. Add beans, then maize. 9. Add coconut milk, stirring occasionally. Simmer until liquid is almost dried up, then remove from heat. 10. Serve as main dish with vegetables.

LUSHORO (MAIZE, BEANS AND MILK)

8 oz (¼ kg) beans

a pinch of bicarbonate of soda

1 teaspoon salt

8 oz (¼ kg) dry maize

4 green bananas

2 pt (1litre) sour milk

2 tablespoons (60 g) butter or ghee

1. Wash and boil maize for about 1 hour, add bicarbonate of soda. 2. Wash beans and add to the cooking maize. 3. Peel bananas, and slice them thinly, and wash them well. 4. Add them into the bens and the maize and cook again until the bananas are cooked and soft. 5. Add in the salt and the butter. 6. Remove from the heat and mash the whole mixture well, dilute with milk to the required consistency. More milk can be used if required. 7. Serve hot or cold as a main dish. *This dish originated from the Msasai people who stay away form home the whole day tending their cattle so they carry it with them in gourds.*

GREEN MAIZE WITH SOUR MILK

8 oz (240 g) green young maize

½ tablespoon butter or margarine

½ lemon, (optional)

1 pt (½litre) sour milk

½ pt (¼litre) water

1. Remove maize from the cobs. 2. Put maize kernels in boiling water. 3. When cooked, drain excess water. Add in fat. 4. Add in sour milk and lemon juice, mix. 5. Serve hot.

NOTE: A pinch bicarbonate of soda added to the boiling maize helps to soften the skin.

GREEN MAIZE AND TOMATOES

4 cobs green maize

4 large tomatoes, sliced

1 onion, chopped

1 dessertspoon (30 g) fat

1. Cut off the maize kernels from cob and mince or pound well. 2. Heat fat in a saucepan and fry onion. 3. Ad tomatoes and cook covered until tender. 4. Add maize and salt. 5. Cook gently or simmer while covered until tender for 20 to 30 minutes. Serve hot.

NOTE: No liquid is needed unless the maize is too mature, in which case a little water may be added.

PUREE (POUNDED MAIZE) WITH SOUR MILK - method 1

4 oz (120 g) pounded maize

¼ pt (1/8litre) sour milk

2 oz (60 g) maize flour

1 oz (30 g) butter, optional

1. Soak maize overnight. 2. Cook in water until soft. 3. Mix maize flour with water to form a soft paste. Add to cooked maize, stir until thick and done. 4. Add butter. Remove from heat, cool slightly and add milk, stir well. 5. Serve warm or cold. The dish is commonly enjoyed by people from Northern Tanzania.

PUREE (POUNDED MAIZE) WITH SOUR MILK - method 2

4 oz (120 g) puree (pounded maize)

½ pt (¼litre) thick sour milk

2 oz (60 g) rice

1 desert spoon butter, (optional)

1. Boil maize until soft. 2. Wash rice and add it to the cooking maize. Continue boiling until very soft. 3. Mash well. The rice grains hold the maize together. 4. Add sour milk and mix it into a thick puree. 5. Serve cold or hot as a main dish.

NOTE: Butter may be added when mashing to enhance flavour.

CORN BREAD (MKATE WA UNGA WA MAHINDI)

4 oz (120 g) maize flour

1 tablespoon sugar

4 level teaspoon baking powder

4 tablespoon butter or margarine

4 oz (120 g) wheat flour

1 level teaspoon slat

2 eggs

water or milk for mixing

Oven temperature

R 4(350 ºF – 175 ºC)

1. Sift all dry ingredients together. 2. Rub butter into the flour mixture. 3. When mixture resembles fine crumbs, stir in beaten egg and enough water to bind to a stiff butter. 4. Pour **butter into** greased (baking) bread tin and bake for about 35 minutes.

CHENGA

1 cup pounded maize

1 cup thick sour milk or yogurt

2 tablespoons maize flour

1. Soak maize overnight. 2. Cook in plenty of water until soft. 3. Make a smooth paste out of maize flour and some water. Add this paste to maize and stir well until it

thickens. 4. Continue to boil until flour is cooked, about 10 minutes. 5. Remove maize from the heat. Leave to cool, then add sour milk. 6. Serve cold.

NOTE: Fresh milk with lemon juice can be used instead of the sour milk or yogurt.

BOILED CASSAVA IN COCONUT MILK

2 lb (1 kg or 2 medium) cassava

1 pt (½liter) thick coconut milk

2 small onions

salt to taste

1. Wash and peel cassava roots. Cut into halves, remove woody pith, then cut into small pieces. Wash cassava again in plenty of water, cook in boiling salted water till half done. 2. Prepare coconut milk. 3. Skin and chop onions very finely. 4. Drain off water from the cooked cassava and add coconut milk, chopped onion and more salt to taste. Stir well till it starts to boil. 5. Lower heat and leave to cook with the lid on for about 10-20 minutes. Do not stir. 6. Serve with meat or chicken and vegetables.

134

CASSAVA CHIPS - method I

16 oz(¼ kg) fresh cassava roots

fat for deep frying

1 teaspoon salt

1. Heat fat for deep frying. 2. Peel cassava roots, slice thinly and wash. 3. Dry in a clean tea towel and fry in hot fat until light frown. 4. Sprinkle with salt and serve hot or cold.

KIMBOYA (MASHED CASSAVA WITH BEANS)

4 oz (120 g) cassava

1 pt (½litre) milk

4 oz (120 gm) beans

a pinch of salt

1. Wash beans and boil until soft. 2. Peel cassava, cut into pieces and wash. 3. Add milk and cassava to beans. Boil gently over low heat until cassava is soft. 4. Mash cassava and beans until soft. 5. Serve hot with vegetables.

COCONUT, BEANS AND CASSAVA

1 medium cassava

½ pt (¼litre) coconut milk

1 onion, chopped

1 tablespoon fat

½ teaspoon curry powder

¼ teaspoon turmeric

1 fresh chilli, chopped

4 oz (120 g) beans

salt to taste

1 tomato, chopped

1. Soak beans overnight. Boil until soft. 2. Prepare coconut milk. 3. Prepare onions, chilli and tomatoes. 4. Peel cassava, remove woody pith and slice. 5. Wash and boil cassava and until soft but firm. 6. Heat fat in a pan and dry onion. Add tomato and spices. 7. Add beans, then coconut milk, stir occasionally. 8. Drain cassava and add to beans. Simmer for about 7-10 minutes. 9. Serve hot with a vegetable.

SORGHUM WITH FRESH BEANS AND CASSAVA (MCHANYATO)

4 oz (120 g) sorghum or white millet

8 oz (240 g or 1 piece cassava)

1 medium onion

½ teaspoon curry powder

1 teaspoon salt

4 oz (120 gm) fresh beans

1 medium tomato

1 clove garlic

1 teaspoon turmeric

½ pt (¼litre) coconut milk

1. Wash and boil sorghum with a little salt. 2. In a separate saucepan, wash and boil beans with a little salt. 3. Peel cassava. Cut into cubes of about 2 inches square. Put them in a saucepan to boil. 4. Peel and chop onion, tomato and garlic, 5. When beans, sorghum and cassava are soft enough, fry onions and garlic in a large saucepan. Add tomatoes and cook till soft. Put in remaining spices, turmeric, curry powder. 6. Strain off water (if any) from beans. Add them to the cooking mixture. Strain off liquid from the sorghum, and add to cooking mixture. Lastly add cassava. Mix all ingredients together, lower heat, and cook for 5 minutes. 7. Add coconut milk, simmer for about 10-15 minutes. 8. Serve hot as a main dish. It can be well eaten with meat stew or fish. This dish is known as *Mchanyato* in Kiswahili, and is common in the coast Region.

CASSAVA FLOUR

as much cassava as required

water for washing and soaking

1. Peel cassava and wash thoroughly. 2. Slice cassava into thin chips. 3. Soak overnight. 4. The following day, drain off water and leave chips on a clean mat or corrugated iron sheet until almost dry. 5. Pound with a mortar or send to millers on the same day. 6. Dry flour for another 2-3 days until very dry, then store in a clean container. 7. This flour is usually used for stiff porridge, thin porridges and in mixture with wheat flour for cakes.

NOTE: The cassava chips must not stay longer than one night in water or they ferment. They also must be dried quickly otherwise they turn black.

DRIED CASSAVA

cassava, any amount

water for washing

1. Peel cassava and wash thoroughly. 2. Slice into thin chips. 3. Spread chips out on a clean mat to dry. 4. Dry thoroughly before storing. 5. Air occasionally.

NOTE: Dried cassava is normally used for pounding into flour. Usual practice is to dry the cassava whole or in large pieces, but this method produces mould cassava due to prolonged state of dampness before it dries.

FRIED BANANAS

2 ripe but firm bananas (*mzuzu* or *mshale*)

2 eggs

sugar to coat, if desired

1 tablespoon milk

fat for shallow frying

1. Beat eggs well and add milk. 2. Peel bananas, split them twice lengthwise, then cut these lengths in half. 3. Heat enough fat to cover the bottom of a frying pan or wide saucepan or *chapati* girdle. 4. Coat each banana piece in turn with the egg and fry on both sides until golden brown. The fat must be moderately hot otherwise, the coating will become hard and rubbery and burns before the bananas are cooked. 5. When golden brown sprinkle with sugar and serve hot for breakfast of a snack.

CHARCOAL ROAST BANANAS

2-3 bananas per person (*mzuzu* or *mshale*)

Butter or high grade ghee or thick cream

1. Light a charcoal stove until red hot. 2. Put a metal wire or bars over the burning charcoal. 3. Peel bananas and arrange them over burning charcoal in such a way that they do not come in direct contact with hot charcoal. 4. Reduce heat by shutting the

stove door and roast at low heat, turning bananas from side to side until they are cooked. 5. When ready, scrape off any part of bananas, which might have turned dark brown or black. 6. Split open bananas lengthwise and spread with a little butter, ghee or cream. 7. Sandwich two halves again and serve hot like baked bananas.

NOTE: The bananas can also be roasted successfully under low grill.

BAKED BANANAS

2-3 roasting bananas per person (*mzuzu* or *mshale*)

butter or high grade ghee

Oven temperature:

R 5 (375 ºF – 175 ºC)

1. Pre-heat oven. 2. Peel bananas and cut off ends. 3. Bake in a hot oven for 20-30 minutes, or until cooked. When ready, bananas should feel soft when pressed. 4. Split cooked bananas open lengthwise, spread with a little butter or ghee. 5. Sandwich the two halves together again and serve hot for a snack, or as a starchy dish to be eaten with vegetable and meat stew.

138

KITAWA (BANANA AND SOUR MILK)

3 small, soft cooking bananas (*Kigoma*, *matoke*, etc)

a little lemon juice, if desired

½ pt (¼litre) thick sour milk or yogurt

a pinch of salt

1. Peel bananas, scrape off their outer film, and split them into two lengthwise. 2. Remove inner pith, then cut lengths twice across. 3. Wash pieces and put to boil. Add salt. 4. When tender, drain off water and mash bananas thoroughly while still hot. 5. Stir in milk a little at a time until all of it has been added. 6. Whisk until smooth. Add lemon juice if used. 7. Serve cold especially for children, invalids and the aged.

GROUNDNUTS WITH BANANAS (KARANGA NA NDIZI)

4 oz (120 g) groundnuts, finely ground

¾ pt (3/8litre) milk

½ oz (15 g) fat

2 ripe bananas

1 oz (30 g) sugar

1. Prepare flour by pounding groundnuts. 2. Peel bananas and slice into neat, equal pieces. 3. Mix groundnuts with milk, add sugar, stir well. 4. Fold in bananas and heat mixture for 5-10 minutes. 5. Serve hot or cold.

BANANA WITH BEANS (MSETO)

3 green bananas

1 large onion, sliced

1 chilli, chopped

½ pt (¼litre) coconut milk

2 oz (120 g) beans

2 medium tomatoes, chopped

½ pt teaspoon turmeric

1 tablespoon (1 oz) fat

1. Wash beans and put in boiling water. 2. Peel and slice bananas, wash. 3. Put in boiling water with salt. 4. Discard water from both beans and bananas. 5. Fry onions, add tomatoes, chilli, curry powder and turmeric. 6. Add in beans and bananas, mix together. 7. Add coconut milk and simmer. Taste for salt. 8. Serve hot with cabbage, spinach, meat or fish.

BANANA YEAST

1 ripe banana (plantain)

1 tablespoonful flour

1 level tablespoon sugar

½ teacup lukewarm water

1. Peel and mash bananas thoroughly. 2. Add sugar, flour and water in turn. 3. Stir well and pour in a bottle. Leave in cool place until it ferments. 4. Use for bread-making or doughnuts.

NOTE: This amount is enough for 1 lb (½ kg) bread.

DRIED BANANAS

semi-ripe bananas

1. Peel bananas and cut them into slices. 2. Put slices on a mat in the sun each day to dry for several days, until the bananas are dry. 3. Alternatively, dry them in a very slow oven for 5-6 hours. 4. When dry, store in a tightly covered container.

NOTE: Do not let bananas get damp or wet. They are better dried over a metal or wooden rack or wire to allow air circulation.

FINGER MILLET PORRIDGE I

4 oz (120 g) finger millet flour

1¼ pt (5/8litre) fresh milk

½ lemon, (optional)

1 tablespoon butter

1 tablespoon sugar

1. Put milk to boil. 2. Mix flour into a smooth paste. 3. Pour hot milk over flour paste and stir well. 4. Return pan to heat, bring to boil while stirring. 5. When porridge is cooked, add butter and lemon juice. Add sugar and stir well. 6. Serve hot for breakfast.

NOTE: Sour milk may be used instead of fresh milk, in which case porridge should be cooked with water. If sour milk is used, sugar becomes optional.
Finger Millet Porridge II

GHEE (PLAIN) CHAPATIS

16 oz (½ kg) flour

1 egg, chopped

enough lukewarm water to mix

4 oz (120 g) ghee or 4 tablespoons oil

½-teaspoon salt

1. Sieve flour and salt into a bowl or pan. 2. Make a well at the centre of the flour. 3. Add a mixture of water and egg, if used. 4. Mix well starting from the centre. 5. When the dough is formed, knead with one tablespoon of fat. 6. Add another tablespoon fat and continue to knead until the dough is smooth. 7. Divide into equal portions depending on size required. 8. Roll each piece into a large round. Generously spread and then roll like a pancake or slit at the radius and roll into cone. Push both ends into seal in fat. Flatten with the palms of your hands. 9. Let aside for 20-30 minutes. 10. Roll out dough to fit the frying pan to be used or to a suitable thickness of about 1/8 inch. 11. Heat frying pan till fairly hot. 12. Fry each chapatti on both sides, until flour sets and it starts to brown. 12. Add a little fat to the pan and finish browning and cooking both sides.

NOTE: On adding, the fat *chapati* should blow up with air bubbles, and brown to a golden colour. 14. Serve hot if possible with green vegetables, meat or fish.

CHAPATI ZA KUMIMINA (SAVOURY PANCAKES)

4 oz (120 g) flour

salt to taste

fat for frying

½ pt (¼litres) milk

1 egg

1. Sieve flour and salt into a bowl. 2. Beat egg add half of the milk. Add flour. Beat until mixture is smooth. 3. Add the rest of the milk and beat. 4. Leave butter to stand for a while. 5. Heat a knob of fat in a frying pan. For each pancake, drop one dessertspoonful of butter onto greased pan. Spread evenly to form nice circles. 6. Lower heat and cook pancakes until brown, then gently turn each one with a spatula or broad-bladed knife, cook undersides. 7. Serve pancakes rolled or placed flat on a plate. They can be served with a beverage or meat and vegetable stews.

COCONUT CHAPATIS

16 oz (½ kg) flour

1 cup coconut milk,

enough to mix flour into a stiff dough

3 oz (120 g) ghee or oil

½ teaspoon salt

1. Make coconut milk from grated coconut. 2. Follow same method as for ghee chapatis, using coconut milk instead of water. As coconut milk contains some fat, the amount of ghee or oil used in the recipe should be reduced. 3. Serve hot or cold with vegetables, meat or fish.

RICE AND VEGETABLE (MSETO)

8 oz (240 g) rice

4 oz (180 g) peas

1 rasher of bacon (optional)

salt to taste

1½ cups water to cook

1 carrot, shredded

1 onion, chopped

1 sweet pepper, finely shredded

½ tablespoon ghee

1. Clean and wash rice. 2. Chop bacon if used. 3. Heat the water. Add salt, onion and fat. 4. Add rice and stir. 5. Wash cabbage and peas. 6. When rice is half cooked, add all the vegetables. 7. Lower heat and cook gently until rice and vegetables are cooked and all water has dried up. 8. Serve hot with meat or fish.

NOTE: Do not overcook the vegetables, they should be crisp when ready.

KICHIRI (MSETO)

8 oz (240 g) rice

1 tomato

½-teaspoon curry powder

1-teaspoon tomato paste

1-tablespoon fat

4 oz (120 g) millet

salt and pepper to taste

1 onion

½-teaspoon turmeric, clove garlic

½ pt (¾lt) coconut milk

1. Soak millet in water for about 4 hours. 2. Boil millet with salt till half-cooked. 3. Wash and soak rice for 15 minutes. 4. Peel and chop onion, garlic and tomato. 5. Melt fat, and fry onion and garlic. Add tomato, fry until soft. Add tomato paste. 6.

Drain water from millet Add millet into frying mixture and cook for about 5 minutes. Add rice and fry together with millet until the rice becomes clear. 7. Add coconut milk, lower heat and cook gently until both rice and millet are well cooked, but not soggy. If coconut milk is not enough, add millet stock. **NOTE:** Do not make it too dry. 8. Garnish with sliced, boiled egg an serve hot a main dish, especially for vegetarians.

GROUNDNUT RICE

4 oz (120 g) groundnuts

2 oz (60 g) fat

½ pt (¼litre) coconut milk

8 oz (¼ kg) rice

salt to taste

½ pt (¼litre) water

1. Fry groundnuts carefully so they don't brown too much. 2. Skin them and coarsely grind them. 3. Soak in water. 4. Prepare and wash rice. Cook in coconut milk, adding more water if necessary. Add soaked groundnuts, salt and fat. Lower heat and cook until rice is done. 5. Serve as a main dish with vegetables.

COCONUT BOILED RICE

8 oz (240 g) rice

½ pt (¼litres) water

1 tablespoon fat

½ pt (¼litres) coconut milk

salt to taste

1 onion, chopped

1. Clean and wash rice, strain. 2. Boil water, add salt and chopped onion. 3. Add coconut milk and fat, continue cooking. 4. Add rice. Reduce heat as soon as rice

begins to boil. Leave to simmer until there is no water but rice is still firm. 5. To finish drying rice, put burning charcoal on a tin over the pan or put the rice in an oven if available. 6. Serve as a starch with stews, vegetables or meat and gravy.

NOTE: Coconut milk much improves the flavour of rice.

RICE FRITTERS

2 oz (60 g) rice

1 small onion, chopped

1 cup water

1 teaspoon baking powder

oil for frying

1 oz (30 g) grated cheese

1 oz (30 g) flour

1 egg

Pepper and salt

1. Clean and wash rice. Bring water to boil, add salt, onion and rice. When rice is almost done, strain off water, leave to cool. 2. Mix together rice, cheese, onion, flour, egg yolk, milk, baking powder, seasoning. 3. Beat egg whites stiff, fold into the mixture 4. From this mixture drop, a tablespoonful at a time into hot fat. Fry until golden brown. Drain on kitchen paper. Serve as snack.

RICE FLOUR

any quantity of rice

water to soak the rice

1. Take some second-grade, cheap rice. 2. Clean by blowing out husks, dust and sand. 3. Wash carefully and soak overnight. 4. Drain water and put rice to partially dry on a clean mat. 5. Pound or send to millers while still damp. 6. Dry damp flour thoroughly on a mat before storing in a container.

NOTE: Rice flour should occasionally be aired even after it has been stored in a container.

CREAMED POTATOES

1 lb (½ kg) potatoes

½ oz (15 g) butter or margarine

1 teaspoon salt

a little hot milk to mix

1. Wash, peel and cook potatoes in salted water. 2. When soft, drain off water and immediately add butter. Mash thoroughly. 3. Add enough hot milk, a little at a time, to make a smooth mixture. 4. Continue to mash potatoes until they are white and fluffy. 5. Serve hot.

CURRIED POTATOES

8 oz (240 gm) potatoes

1 teaspoon lemon juice

½ teaspoon turmeric

salt to taste

a pinch of chill powder

½ teaspoon coriander seeds

1 small onion, chopped

1 teaspoon chopped parsley or *kotimiri*

1 tablespoon ghee or other fat

1 clove garlic, crushed

cinnamon powder

1 teaspoon tomato paste

1. Wash, peel and dice potatoes coarsely. 2. Heat fat in a pan and fry onions and garlic for a while. 3. Add potatoes, lemon juice tomato paste and all other ingredients; let mixture cook for a few minutes before adding water. 4. Cook covered until potatoes are cooked and the liquid almost dried. 5. Serve hot.

POTATO CHIPS

½ lb (240 g) potatoes

fat for deep frying

1 level teaspoon salt

1. Wash and peel potatoes. 2. Chip potatoes thinly or cut into fingers. 3. Wipe chips with a clean cloth. 4. Heat fat in a pan or frying pan until hot. 5. Fry chips in small lots quickly until cooked light coloured and crisp. 6. Toss them in a little salt and serve hot.

NOTE: It is advisable to fry chips in small quantities to avoid cooling the fat too much.

SWEET POTATO BALLS

½ lb (240 g) sweet potatoes

2 eggs

Fat for shallow frying

1 oz (30 g) flour

salt and pepper to taste

1. Wash potatoes, peel and boil until cooked. 2. Drain off water and mash thoroughly. Add seasoning and beaten egg. 3. Form into small balls and roll these in flour to coat. 4. Heat fat in a pan or frying pan and fry the balls until light brown. 5. Drain well and serve hot or cold for snacks.

YAM PORRIDGE

1 medium yam

a pinch of salt

½ pt (¼ litre) fresh milk

sugar to taste, (optional)

1. Wash yam and bail in its skin until tender. 2. When yam is cooked, peel the skin off.
3. Grate yam even finely, add salt, then stir thoroughly, adding the milk little at a time.
Add sugar if used. 4. When ready, the mixture should be thick and creamy. 5. Serve
cold.

FUTARI YAMS

¼ lb (240 g) yam

½ teaspoon curry powder

1 tomato

salt to taste

½ cup groundnuts, ground

1 onion

1 tablespoon oil or ghee

water to cook

1. Scrub yams and boil until cooked. 2. Slice onion and tomato. 3. Heat fat in a pan.
Fry onions and tomato. 4. Add seasonings and groundnuts. 5. Peel and slice yams.
Add to groundnut mixture. Add water to reach the same level as the mixture. 6. Bring
to boil, then lower heat and simmer for 15 minutes, adding more water if necessary.
7. When ready the mixture should be like a thick, whole maize porridge. 8. Serve hot
with meat and vegetables.

YAMS IN TOMATO AND ONION SAUCE

2 medium yams

1 large onion

salt to taste

2 teaspoons lemon juice

3 tomatoes

1 tablespoon fat

1 teaspoon curry powder

water to boil

1. Wash, peel and cut yams into even-sized pieces. 2. Boil in salted water until tender. 3. Peel and chop onions, 4. Skin and slice tomatoes. 5. Heat fat in a pan. Add onions, seasonings and lemon juice. 6. Fry at low heat until tomatoes and onions are tender. 8. Add cooked yams to tomato sauce. Stir and continue to cook for another 5-10 minutes. 9. When ready there should be very little liquid left. 10 Serve hot.

ROAST SWEET POTATOES

2 lb (1 kg) sweet potatoes

fat for roasting

1. Wash and peel potatoes. 2. Cut into circles or lengthwise, as preferred. 3. Boil until half cooked. 4. Drain water, add potatoes. 5. Add fat and put into a tin, roast in a preheated oven, basting from time to time until potatoes are cooked and brown. Serve hot with meat.

MASHED SWEET POTATOES

1 lb (½ kg) sweet potatoes

1 small onion, chopped

1 oz (30 g) butter or margarine

a little milk to mix

1. Wash, peel and boil potatoes. Add onions to the boiling water. 2. When potatoes are cooked, drain off excess water. Add butter and mash thoroughly. 3. Add enough hot milk to make potatoes smooth. 4. Serve hot. 5. Turn into a baking dish and brown in a hot oven, then serve.

SWEET POTATO CHIPS

½ lb (240 g) sweet potatoes

fat for deep frying

1 level teaspoon salt

Follow the same method as for potato chips.

CASSAVA CHIPS - method 2

½ lb (240 g) cassava root

fat for deep-frying

a pinch of salt

1. Peel and chip cassava. 2. Put to boil in salt water until half done. 3. Drain and wipe dry with a clean cloth. 4. Heat fat in a pan and fry chips until crisp and light-brown coloured. 5. Serve hot.

YAM FLOUR

As many yams as desired

1. Peel yams and wash. 2. Slice into thin chips. Put to dry on a clean mat or corrugated iron sheet until fairly dry. (This may take 2-3 days). 3. During the night leave chips spread on the mat and never store in a container unless dry. 4. Pound with a mortar or send to local millers. 5. Dry the flour for a day or two then store and use as required. 6. The flour can be used in the same way as maize flour.

7
EGGS

SCRAMBLE EGGS

egg(s)

salt and pepper

a little fat

1 tablespoon milk

1. Break egg into a bowl, add a pinch of salt and pepper. 2. Beat with a fork until all traces of ropiness are removed. 3. Stir in milk. 4. Melt a teaspoon of fat in frying pan but do not allow it to brown or haze. 5. Add egg and cook gently, stirring all the time, until the mixture is almost set but still creamy. **NOTE:** If overcooked, egg will become tough and hard, and a watery liquid will separate out. 6. Serve on buttered toast or with a slice of tomato.

POACHED EGGS

egg(s)

water

salt

1. Half fill a frying pan with water. 2. Bring water to boil and add 1 teaspoon salt for every pint of water. 3. Break egg into a saucer and slide into boiling water. 4. Simmer but do not boil for 5 minutes, or until white is opaque. 5. Lift out with a skimmer, spatula or fish slicer, drain well. 6. Serve on hot buttered toast.

NOTE: A neat shape can be obtained by sliding the egg into a greased plain biscuit cutter placed in the frying pan.

FRIED STUFFED EGGS

2 eggs, hard-boiled

1 tablespoon fat

1 tablespoon flour

1 tablespoon minced meat

1 teaspoon chopped parsley

1 small onion, chopped

1 teaspoon lemon juice

pepper and salt to taste

beaten egg and breadcrumbs for coating

fat for deep frying

1. Half hard-boiled eggs lengthwise and remove yolks. 2. Melt fat, fry onion then meat. 3. Stir in flour, add milk and boil gently for 2 minutes. 4. Chop egg yolks. Add to sauce egg yolks, parsley, lemon juice and seasoning, mix well. 5. Fill egg whites with mixture, coat first with beaten egg, then breadcrumbs. 6. Fry in hot fat golden brown, drain on paper. Serve as snack or as protein dish in a full.

8
FRUITS AND SWEETS

STEWED PAWPAW

1 small pawpaw, hard but yellow

2-3 tablespoons sugar

juice of ½ lemon

a pinch of ginger

1. Peel pawpaw and remove seeds. 2. Slice into neat pieces. 3. Put pieces in a pan. Add enough water to half cover the pawpaws. 4. Add sugar and lemon juice, simmer until pawpaws are soft. 5. When ready serve cold with cream, if available.

STEWED MAPERA (GUAVAS)

1 lb *mapera*

2 cups water

6 tablespoons sugar

Lemon rind (optional)

1. Wash, peel and remove seeds from the fruit. 2. Bring water and sugar plus rind to boil. Cook until syrupy. 3. Add prepared fruit, simmer until tender. 4. Place fruit in a dish and pour over the syrup. If syrup is too thin, cook to reduce the quantity of water in an open pan.

STEWED MANGO

2-3 large mangoes, hard but yellow

3 tablespoons sugar

a piece of cinnamon bark

1. Peel mangoes and slice from their seeds. 2. Place mangoes on a pan. Add enough water to half cover mangoes. 3. Add sugar and cinnamon and simmer until mangoes are soft. Remove cinnamon bark. 4. Serve hot or cold with cream, if available.

GROUNDNUT KASHATA - method I

(For three persons)

4 oz (120 g) groundnuts, roasted and peeled

2½ oz (75 g) sugar

a little cinnamon

1. Make syrup. Put sugar in a frying pan. Melt sugar over low heat. When it starts to dissolve, stir with a wooden spoon until sugar starts to brown. Add in groundnuts and cinnamon and stir until mixture starts to harden. 2. While mixture is still hot but soft, pour onto a sugared board. 3. Press mixture flat to a thickness of about ¼" 4 inches .Using a sharp knife, cut into pieces before mixture is cool. 5. Lift pieces with a pallete or other knife onto a plate to avoid sticking to the board. **NOTE:** The shelled groundnuts may be coarsely chopped before use.

GROUNDNUT KASHATA - method 2

4 oz (120 g) groundnuts, roasted and shelled

4 oz (120 g) sugar

oil for brushing the board

1. Brush pastry board with oil. 2. Melt sugar into syrup (see groundnut *kashata* method 1). 3. Add in groundnuts and mix quickly. 4. Pour mixture into pastry board. Level the surface with rolling pin or knife. 5. Cut into square or make round balls. 6. Serve cold with coffee.

COCONUT KASHATA

4 oz (120 g) grate dried coconut

3 oz (90 g) sugar

a pinch of cinnamon

1. Grate coconut and dry it. 2. Melt sugar in a pan. 3. Add coconut. 4. Cook, stirring occasionally until the sugar turns light brown and reaches setting point. 5. Remove pan from heat and spread mixture on a board. 6. Roll it slightly to required thickness, cut into even cubes and leave to set. 7. Serve with tea, coffee or other beverage or as a snack.

155

CASHEWNUT KASHATA

4 oz (120 g) cashewnuts, whole split or chopped

4 oz (120 g) sugar

oil to grease pastry board

1.Grease pastry board with oil or fat. 2. Melt sugar until it changes to light brown syruo. 3. Add nuts and stir mixture quickly until nuts are bound together. 4.Put mixture on pastry board, level and spread with a knife then divide into required shapes. (Do this quickly before mixture is harned). 5.Serve as a snack

SWEET COCONUT RICE PUDDING

3 oz (90gm) rice

¼ pint (1/8 lt) coconut milk

1 oz (30 gm) sugar

1 oz (30 gm) margarine

1 pint (½ litre) milk

1. Collect ingredients, sugar, rice, milk and coconut milk. 2. Wash rice and soak. 3. Add milk, sugar and margarine. 4. Cook at very low heat until rice is almost done (1½ hours). 5. Add in coconut milk, cook for another ½ hour. 6. Serve hot or cold. **NOTE:** The pudding can be baked instead of simmering.

GREEN MAIZE PUDDING

1 cup green maize, very young

1 tablespoon honey

½ pt (¼ litre) fresh milk

2 drops vanilla essence food colouring, (optional)

Oven temperature:

R 2 (300 ºF – 150 ºC)

1. Pre-heat oven. 2. Pound or mince maize grain. 3. Grease a baking dish. 4. Add in milk, honey, vanilla essence and food colouring and mix well. Add maize. 5. Bake in a slow oven on the middle shelf for 1-1¼ hours. When ready it should set and a light brown coat formed on top. 6. Serve cold as a sweet for lunch or dinner.
NOTE: If maize is not very young (i.e. it is a bit hard) then boil it first in milk for about 15-20 minutes and then finish cooking in oven.

GREEN MAIZE WITH CUSTARD

2 cobs green maize

½ pt (¼ litre) milk

1 egg

1 teaspoon sugar

Oven temperature

R 3 (325 °F – 165 °C)

1. Remove maize from cob and wash. 2. Mince or pound the maize well. 3. Beat up eggs, add sugar and milk. 4. Add maize to egg custard. 5. Pour into greased fireproof dish. 6. Bake until set for 1 hour.

PUMPKIN CUSTARD

12 oz (360 g) pumpkins, cooked and mashed

4 large eggs

1 pt (½ litre) milk

a little margarine for greasing

a little ground cinnamon (*mdalasini*)

2 oz (60 g or tablespoons) sugar

Oven temperature

R 3 (325 °F)

1. Break eggs and beat well. 2. Add milk, then strain. 3. Mix the custard (egg and milk), sugar and pumpkin, and stir well. 4. Pour pumpkin mixture into greased oven-proof dish. Sprinkle with cinnamon. 5. Bake in pre-heated oven. 6. Bake for 1-1½ hours or until the custard is set, depending on the depth of the custard. 7. Custard can be steamed instead of baking. 8. Serve as sweet (dessert) or as dish for invalids or children.

NOTE: The pumpkin used in this dish should be matured, those starting to turn yellowish in colour.

PINEAPPLE CHOCOLATE PUDDING

1 slice (ring) fresh pineapple

½ mango, (optional)

1 tablespoon sugar

4 tablespoons pineapple juice

vanilla essence

1 oz (30 g) chocolate or 1 tablespoon cocoa powder

¼pt (⅛ litre) milk

1 tablespoon cocoa powder

1 round teaspoon corn flour

1. Peel pineapple and cut into small neat cubes. 2. Wash, peel and cut mango (if used). 3. Put fruit in a serving dish. 4. Take remaining bits of pineapple, mash them and strain juice into a pan. 5. Add sugar and heat pan over low heat to dissolve all sugar. 6. Pour sweetened fruit juice over fruits. 7. Prepare chocolate. Mix cornflower into a taste with 1 tablespoon of cold milk. Boil rest of the milk. Add chocolate (or cocoa powder) and stir carefully till all have dissolved. Add cornflower paste and stir well (use wooden spoon to avoid forming lumps, until mixture begins to thicken). 8. Pour chocolate mixture over fruits and leave to cool for a while, then put in refrigerator or a bowl with cold water and cover till served. 9. Serve cold as a sweet.

GOURD PUDDING

12 oz (360 g) young gourd

¼ pt (⅛ litre) milk

1 oz (30 g) sugar

1 oz (30 g) raisins

1 egg

1 orange

Oven temperature

R 4 (350 ºF – 175 ºC)

1. Peel and cut ground into small pieces, removing excess seeds. 2. Wash and cook in a little water till very tender. 3. Grate rind of orange and squeeze out juice. 4. Put rind and juice in a pan, add sugar and bring to boil for 2-3 minutes. 5. Pre-heat oven. 6. Drain water from gourds and mash them thoroughly. 7. Break and beat and add to milk. Rinse raisins with water. 8. Add milk and egg mixture to gourd and mix well. Add raisins. 9. Add orange juice and rind, mix well. Pour into greased baking dish and bake for 25-30 minutes on middle shelf, till set. 10. Serve decorate with glace cherries as a sweet, or invalid or child's dish.

AVOCADO MILK PUDDING

1 medium riped avocado

½ pt (¼ litre) milk or a little cream

sugar to taste

a slice of ripe mango, for decoration

1. Wash, peel and cut avocado into neat cubes. 2. Arrange them in serving dish. 3. Cut up slice of mango and add into serving dish. 4. Sprinkle with sugar and pour in milk or cream. 5. Serve for breakfast or as a second course.

NOTE: 1) Other fruits such as pawpaw, orange, etc, can also be used to provide good colour instead of mango. 2) This dish is also good for children, especially for its nutritive value.

FRUIT TIER PUDDING

Sweet pastry

3½ oz (105 g) plain flour

2 egg yolks

2 oz (60 g) margarine

1½ oz (45 g) icing sugar

Custard sauce

1 tablespoon custard powder

1 tablespoon sugar

1/2 pint (1/4 litre) milk

Meringue

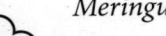

2 egg whites

3 oz (90 g) castor sugar

1 large ripe mango1 ring of pineapple

1 small tin (170 g) cream

1 small tin (170 g) cream

Oven temperature

R6 (400 °F – 200 °C) then R3 (325 °F – 165 °C)

1. Heat oven. 2. Make pastry and roll out into shape of the baking dish. Bake blind for 20-25 minutes. 3. Prepare filling. Peel and cut pineapple into small, equal cubes. Wash and cut up mango, removing the core. Slice. Mix sliced mango with cream and beat well. 4. Take pastr4y out of oven, leave to cool and lower oven temperature. 5. Prepare custard sauce and mix with the pineapples. Pour the mixture into flan case.

6. Put mango and cream mixture on top of the custard. 7. Prepare the meringue: Put egg whites (yolks were used to mix the pastry) in clean, grease-free bowl. Whisk until egg whites are fluffy and stand up in peaks. Gradually fold in sugar very gently with a metal tablespoon, being careful not to knock out the entrapped air. 8. Pile meringue on top of pastry filling. Bake pastry in oven for about 30 minutes, until meringue is firm and crisp. 9. Serve hot or cold as a sweet.

BANANA FOOL

2 ripe bananas

½ pt (¼ litre) milk

1 tablespoon (1 litreoz) custard powder

2 tablespoons (oz) sugar

1. Mix custard powder and a little milk to make a smooth thin paste. Heat remaining milk. When hot but not boiling, add slowly, to the custard in a bowl, stirring all the time with a wooden spoon. Add sugar. 3. Return this mixture to saucepan. 4. Cook slowly, stirring all the time until it thickens. Continue to cook until starch is cooked. 5. Leave custard to cool. 6. Meanwhile, peel and mash bananas and pass through a sieve, if necessary. 7. Pour cold custard over mashed bananas and whisk until mixture is light in texture. 8. Pour into a sweet dish decorated with lemon rind or invalid. **NOTE:** Other fruit pulps can be used for making fools, e.g. guava, apricots, mangoes, peaches.

TAMBI (SWEET VERMICELLI) - METHOD I

4 oz (120 g) vermicelli

2 tablespoons sugar

1 tablespoon (30 g) fat

2 cardamom pods

2 pints water, plus 3 tablespoons

1. Boil water in a saucepan. 2. Dip the vermicelli in boiling water and leave to boil for 15 minutes or until cooked but not soggy. 3. Drain vermicelli through a colander or sieve. 4. Meanwhile, pour about three tablespoons water in a saucepan. Add the fat and when it starts boiling, stir in the cardamom seeds and sugar. Stir until it dissolves completely. Add the cooked vermicelli. **NOTE:** This dish is normally served hot with a beverage or during religious fasting periods.

TAMBI (SWEET VERMICELLI) - METHOD 2

4 oz (120 g) *tambi*

2 oz (60 g) sugar

1 tablespoon fat

a pinch of cinnamon

1 cardamom pod

1. Boil *tambi* in water until soft. Set aside. 2. Heat fat in a pan and add cinnamon and cardamom. 3. Fry them together until mixture is brown. 4. Stir in *tambi* and add to spice mixture, add sugar and stir well. Cook for about 5-7 minutes. 5. When cool, serve.

LIVER SWEET

¼ pt (⅛ litre) milk

1 level tablespoon custard powder

1 level tablespoon sugar

4 oz (120 g) minced liver

1. Wash, skin and cut liver into small cubes. Mince the liver. 2. Remove all the pieces from the mincer, boil in just enough water to cook the liver for bout 10 minutes.
3. Mix custard powder with 2 teaspoons of milk in a bowl. 4. Boil the rest of the milk with sugar, stirring all the time. 5. Pour the boiled milk into the custard paste, stirring with a wooden spoon. 6. Rinse the pan in cold water. 7. Return the mixture into the

pan, boil for about 5 minutes until the mixture thickens and cook, avoiding lumps. 8. Add minced liver and stir well. 9. Serve warm for an invalid or growing child.

RICE AND COCONUT PORRIDGE

4 oz (120 g) rice

2 oz (60 g) sugar

1 grated coconut

a pinch of cinnamon

water

1. Wash rice, remove sand and soak for one hour. 2. Meanwhile prepare one-cup thick coconut milk and 2 cups thin coconut milk from the grated coconut milk. 3. Gently simmer rice in this coconut milk until very soft. 4. Add thick coconut milk, cinnamon and sugar and continue to simmer for 10 minutes. Stir occasionally. 5. When ready, porridge should be thick and creamy. 6. Serve hot or cold. Especially suitable for children, invalids and the aged.

PEPETA (FRIED RICE AND GROUNDNUTS)

8 oz (¼ kg) rice

6 oz (180 g) groundnuts

4 oz (120 g) sugar

fat for frying

1. Wash rice and soak overnight. 2. Drain water and dry rice with clean towel. 3. Wash groundnuts and dry them. 4. Heat fat in a deep pan or frying pan until hot. 5. Fry nuts and the rice together until both are cooked. 6. Drain off any surplus fat and sprinkle with sugar. 7. Cool before serving as a snack, or store in polythene bags.

RICE DOUGHNUTS (VITUMBUA)

2 oz (60 g) wheat flour

8 oz (240 g) *rice flour* or

1 teaspoon yeast or 1 tablespoon *chibuku* brew

½ level teaspoon or *ground cinnamon*

4 oz (120 g) sugar

½ pt (½ cup) water

oil for shallow frying

a little milk for creaming the yeast

1. Add cinnamon to rice and whet flours, sift into a large mixing bowl. Add sugar. 2. Warm the water. 3. Make a thick batter with flour mixture and water. 4. Cream yeast with a little warm milk and sugar. Leave to dissolve. 5. Add the yeast (or *chibuku*) to batter. Stir well until the batter produces air bubbles. 6. Leave batter covered for at least six hours or until it rises and produces a lot of air bubbles. 7. Heat a little fat in a large frying pan. Fry the batter in tablespoonfuls, spreading a little to form a good shape and even thickness. 8. Fry on both sides until cooked and golden brown. 9. Drain off excess fat, roll in sugar, if desired. Serve for snacks or packed meals.

164

MAHANDO

4 oz (120 g) wheat flour

a pinch of salt

1 teaspoon baking powder

fat for deep frying

cold water for mixing

1 oz (30 g or 1 tablespoon) fat

Sugar syrup

2 tablespoons (60 g) sugar

¼ pint (⅛ litre) water

1. Sieve flour, baking powder and salt into a mixing bowl. 2. Rub in fat. Add water and mix to a soft dough. 3. Divide dough into 4 portions. Roll each portion separately on to a floured board making oblongs on circles about ¼" thick. 4. Pull two opposite ends of each dough portion, using a finger and thumb, to centre to form shape of a butterfly. 5. Fry dough butterflies in very hot fat for 3 or 4 minutes. Make sure that they are not too brown. 6. Make syrup: Warm sugar and water slowly. Water should not boil until all sugar has dissolve. 7. Glaze the *mahande* with syrup.

JAM BUNS

8 oz (240 g) flour

2 level tablespoons custard powder

2 teaspoons baking powder

2 oz (60 g) margarine

2 oz (60 g) sugar

8-10 tablespoons milk

some jam

Oven temperature:

R 5 (435 ºF – 175 ºC)

1. Sift flour, custard powder into a bowl. 2. Rub fat into flour. Add sugar and mix well with a knife. 3. Add milk and mix into a stiff dough. 4. Divide dough into 16-20 equal portions. 5. Place balls on a greased baking sheet. 6. Make a little hole on each ball with your finger and put a little jam in it. 7. Bake in fairly hot oven, for 20 to 25 minutes or until cooked and light brown.

COCONUT BALLS

4 oz (120 g) flour

2 oz (60 g) margarine

2 oz (60 g) sugar

2 oz (60 g) fresh grated coconut

½ an egg

⅛ pint milk

1 teaspoon baking powder

Oven temperature:

R (400 ºF – 200 ºC)

1. Sieve the flour with baking powder. 2. Rub fat in the flour with your finger tips. 3. Add sugar and half of the grated coconut. 4. Mix into a fairly stiff dough with egg and milk. 5. Roll mixture in small balls. Roll over remaining grated coconut and put on a greased baking sheet. 6. Bake in oven for 15 minutes.

NOTE: Dry the coconut a bit after grating it.

VIMANDA (BANANA AND RICE BALLS)

3 ripe bananas

(20 g) rice flour

1 egg

1 tablespoon milk, (optional)

1 oz (30 g) sugar, if desired

a little nutmeg

1. Peel bananas and put them in a bowl. 2. Mash them thoroughly, add in rice flour, sugar and nutmeg and mix well together with beaten egg. 3. Divide mixture into four equal portions. Dredge these with a little flour and roll them into balls. 4. Cover each

ball completely with aluminum foil paper in such a way that no water will penetrate inside during boiling. 5. Boil the balls in water for 20 to 30 minutes. 6. Remove foil paper and serve vimanda with a beverage. *The balls are traditionally boiled wrapped in banana or other vegetable leaves.*

PINEAPPLE FRITTERS

4 oz (120 g) flour

1 egg

a pinch of salt

½ pt (¼ litre) milk, to mix

1 level teaspoon baking powder

6 rings of large ripe pineapple, ¼-½ thick each

sugar for coating

fat for deep fat frying

1. Make a coating batter from flour egg, salt and baking powder, as for banana fritters. 2. Heat fat until hot. 3. Dry each pineapple ring with a clean dry cloth or absorbent paper to remove excess water. 4. Turn rings in batter, then fry in hot fat until golden brown. 5. Drain on a rack and while hot coat with sugar spread on a kitchen paper or plate. 6. Serve hot or cold for snack.

BREAD AND JAM FRITTERS

2 oz (60 g) flour

½ cup (¼pt or ⅛ litre) milk

¼ teaspoon baking powder

4 standard slices bread (stale bread is more suitable)

1 egg

2 tablespoons jam

fat for deep frying

1. Make a coating batter as for banana fritters. 2. Make two sandwiches from bread and jam. 3. Heat fat until hot. 4. Cut each sandwich into either two strips or four squares. 5. Dip sandwich pieces into batter with extra care so as not to separate bread pieces. 6. Fry sandwich pieces in fat until golden brown. 7. Drain on a cooling rack and while still warm coat with sugar. 8. Serve hot for snack.

BANANA FRITTERS

4 oz (120 g) flour

1 egg

a pinch of salt

½ pt (¼ litre) milk, to mix

1 level teaspoon baking powder

6 ripe but firm bananas

sugar for coating

fat for deep frying

1. Make a coating batter from flour, egg, milk, salt and baking powder. Follow the method as for Banana Drop Scones. 2. Peel bananas and cut them into halves length-wise, and turn them into batter on a plate. 3. Heat the fat until fairly hot, add coasted bananas and fry until golden brown. 4. Drain on a rock and while hot coat with sugar spread on a kitchen paper or plate. 5. Serve hot with lemon wedges for snack.

MANGO FRITTERS

3 oz (90 g) flour

1 egg

3 tablespoons milk

½ oz (15 g) sugar

1 medium mango

fat for deep frying

1. Make the batter. Sieve flour into a bowl and add sugar. Break egg and beat. Mix with milk and pour into flour gradually. Mix it well into a coating consistency. 2. Wash and peel mango. Cut into small neat pieces. 3. Heat oil in a deep frying pan. 4. Coat mango pieces with batter and fry till golden brown. 5. Drain on an absorbent paper. 6. Sprinkle with sugar (if desired) and serve hot or cold as sweet for lunch, dinner or snack.

BANANA DROPS

2 ripe sweet bananas

2 oz (60 g) plain wheat flour

2 oz (60 g) *sembe* or rice flour

1 level tablespoon custard powder

1 rounded teaspoon baking powder

1 oz (30 g) margarine

½ oz (15 g) sugar, (optional)

3-4 tablespoons milk

juice of ½ lemon

½ oz (15 g) raisins, chopped

fat or oil for deep frying

1. Peel and wash bananas. Add lemon juice and mash well. 2. Mix plain and *sembe* flour, custard powder and baking powder and sieve into a mixing bowl. 3. Rub in margarine till it is well distributed throughout the mixture. 4. Add sugar and raisins. 5. Pour mashed bananas into flour mixture; add milk and beat well with a wooden spoon. 6. Heat oil in a deep frying pan. 7. Using a tablespoon, drop spoonful of batter into hot fat. Cook drops until golden brown. 8. Drain on absorbent paper and serve hot or cold with tea.

BANANA DROP SCONES

4 oz (120 g) flour

1 egg

1 cup (¼ litre) milk or water to mix

4 sweet ripe bananas

1-2 oz (30-60g) sugar

4-6 tablespoons oil for frying

1. Peel and mash bananas thoroughly; if necessary pass them through a course sieve. Add sugar, 2. Make a batter from flour, egg and milk or water as follow: Sieve flour into a bowl. Beat egg, add some of the milk. Make a well at the centre of the flour, pour in the egg mixture and stirring from the centre with a wooden spoon incorporate in all the flour. Add remaining milk or water. 3. Add mashed bananas and stir well. 4. Heat fat in large heavy frying pan until fairly hot. 5. Drop spoonful of banana mixture into fat, smooth them down into circles with back of the spoon. 6. Fry both sides to a golden brown. 7. Serve hot or cold for snacks. **NOTE:** Drop scones cooked in fat, which is too cool, will be soggy and greasy.

COCONUT BUNS

4 oz (120 g) flour

2 oz (60 g) dried coconut, grated

2 oz(60 g) margarine

2 oz (60 g) sugar

1 egg

2 level teaspoons baking powder

a little milk for mixing

Oven temperature

R 5(425 ºF – 215 ºC)

1. Sieve flour and baking powder into a bowl. 2. Rub in margarine. 3. Add sugar and coconut, mix well. 4. Add beaten egg with milk, mix to form dough. 5. Divide dough into 10 equal parts and roll them into balls. 6. Roll each ball in grated dried coconut. Bake balls on greased baking sheet for about 10-15 minutes.

BANANA BREAD

2 teacups flour

1 level cup sugar

1 level cup margarine

1 teaspoonful baking powder

2 ripe bananas

½ cup milk

2 eggs

Oven temperature:

R 4 (350 ºF – 175 ºC)

1. Cream margarine and sugar together until soft and creamy. 2. Beat eggs and add milk. 3. Sieve flour, baking powder and salt together. 4. Thoroughly mash bananas and if necessary pass through a sieve. 5. Gradually add egg to flour then stir in mashed bananas. 6. Grease a bread tin, dust with flour and pour in banana mixture. 7. Bake in moderate oven for 1 - 1¼ hours. 8. To test for readiness, stick a blunt knife through the bread. It should come out clean.

BANANA CAKES (MABUMUNDA OR VIMANDA)

Makes 4 cakes in ordinary cups.

4 ripe bananas

2 oz (60 g) fine *sembe* flour, preferably home pounded

1 oz (30 g) margarine

½ oz (15 g) sugar (optional)

1 egg

1. Put water to boil in a large steamer. 2. Peel and wash the bananas. 3. Sieve flour and rub in fat. Add sugar. 4. Mix flour with bananas and beat well to a soft dough. Add well-beaten egg. 5. Grease steaming bowls or cups and then add mixture to the bowls or cups to about three-quarters full. 6. Cover with kitchen paper (grease proof paper), tie well and put in the steamer. 7. Steam for about 1-1½ hours. 8. When ready turn quickly on to a cooling tray.

NOTE: Banana cakes are a good item for journeys but must first be dried in the seen for sometime. If well-kept they last for about one week. The cakes can also be fried in bananas leave which have been warmed lightly over fire and then cooked in a pan of boiling water instead of a steamer.

PEACH HATS

½ lb (¼ kg) fresh peaches

½ oz (15 g) sugar

4 oz (120 g) plain flour

2 oz (60 g) margarine

a pinch of salt

cold water

Over temperature

R 5-6 (475 ºF – 250 ºC)

1. Prepare short crust pastry. Sift flour and salt into a mixing bowl. Rub in fat with the fingertips till mixture is like breadcrumbs. Add cold water (about 3-4 tablespoon). Bind lightly with the fingers but do not knead. Cover dough and leave to set in a cool place. Pre-heat oven. 3. Grease baking sheet. 4. Wash and peel peaches. Cut them in half and remove stones. 5. Sprinkle peach halves with sugar. 6. Roll out pastry to 1/8 inches thickness and 3" diameter, using a pastry-cutter. Cut out pastry into pairs of

rounds. 7. Put one peach half on each round and damp the edges with water. Cover peaches with second round of pastry and seal the edges well. Repeat this process until all peaches and pastry are finished. 8. Put them on baking sheet and bake in hot oven, top shelf for 20-25 minutes (pastry should be light brown when done). 9. Serve cold for morning or afternoon tea. Also good for children's parties and snacks.

PEACH CRUMBLE

½ lb (¼ kg) fresh peaches

1 oz (30 g) sugar

2 oz (60 g) plain flour

1 oz (30 g) margarine

2 teaspoons cinnamon

3 almond nuts or cashew nuts

2 tablespoons water

Oven temperature

R 5(375 ºF – 185 ºC)

1. Pre-heat oven. 2. Wash and peel peaches. Cut them into slices and discard seeds. 3. Put them in baking dish and sprinkle with half the sugar, add water and sprinkle with some cinnamon. 4. Prepare crumble. Sieve flour and about ½ teaspoon cinnamon. Rub fat into flour until it looks like breadcrumbs. Chop nuts and add them to the mixture and sprinkle a bit more cinnamon. 6. Bake in hot oven for 25-30 minutes on top shelf, until fruit is cooked and crumble is golden brown.

MAIZE SWEET (MTAMU WA UNGA WA MAHINDI)

8 oz (240 g) maize flour

4 oz (120 g) sugar

1 egg

1 pt ½ litre) milk

2 tablespoons (60 g) butter ground cinnamon, (optional)

Oven temperature

R 4 (350 ℉ – 175 ℃)

1. Sift all dry ingredients into a bowl. 2. Add sugar. 3. Beat eggs, and milk, beat well and add melted butter. 4. Add a little amount of liquid into dry ingredients and mix well. 5. Pour mixture into greased dish and bake in moderately hot oven for 2 hours. 6. Serve hot or cold.

PAWPAW CAKES

¼ ripe medium-sized pawpaw (depending on variety of pawpaw)

3 oz (90 g) flour

½ oz (15 g) sugar

1 oz (30 g) fat

1 rounded teaspoon baking powder

1 egg

1 tablespoon milk, (optional)

Oven temperature:

R 6 (400 ℉ – 200 ℃)

1. Pre-heat oven. 2. Greased a twelve-patty tin and dust it lightly with flour. 3. Peel and mash pawpaw. Add milk and egg and beat well. 4. Sieve flour and baking powder into a mixing bowl. 5. Rub in fat until mixture looks like fine breadcrumbs. 6. Add sugar. 7. Pour pawpaw mixture into flour and mix well to a soft consistency. If mixture is a bit stiff, add more milk. 8. Put one tablespoon of mixture into each patty tin. 9. Bake in oven on top shelf for 20-25 minutes.

CHINA GRASS

a bundle can be used per 4 pints
litre of milk or juice or pulp

Mango sweet

¼ bundle of China grass
¾ pt of water
4 oz sugar
1 tin mango pulp

Milk sweet

¼ bundle of China Grass
¾ pt of water
4 oz sugar
1 pint milk
vanilla essence
food colouring (optional)

1. Heat together water and China grass until it dissolves. 2. Strain and mix with sugar, stir well until sugar dissolves. 3. Add mango pulp (or milk and vanilla). Put mixture in a mould and keep in cool place to set. Refrigeration is not necessary.

NOTE: Mango or orange juice can be used instead of mango pulp.

APPLE IN MOULD

½ lb (¼ kg) fresh apples
4 glace cherries
1 tablespoon lemon juice
1 dessert spoon sugar

1½ (45 g) corn flour

1 pt (½ litre) milk

1 oz (30 g) sugar

vanilla essence

food colouring (optional)

1. Put cold water in serving dish (fancy mould). 2. Wash, peel and dice apples. Sprinkle them with lemon juice and sugar. 3. Cut cherries into small pieces and mix then with apples. 4. Prepare corn flour. Mix corn flour powder with a bit of cold milk to make a paste. Boil the rest of the milk. Add sugar, vanilla essence and colouring. Add milk to corn flour paste, stirring with a wooden spoon. Rinse out pan in cold water and return the mixture to the pan. Put it back to cook for 3 minutes, stirring all the time to avoid forming lumps. 5. Remove from heat and very quickly add in diced apples and cherries and mix well. 6. Pour water from the mould and pour in corn flour mixture. 7. Put in a cool place to cool first, and then keep in refrigerator for 1 hour or more to set. Alternatively, set mould in a basin of cold water. 8. Turn out after mixture has cooled, onto a plate and decorate with pineapple cubes. (The dish of mould can also be served in the mould in which it is prepared). 9. Serve as a sweet.

AVOCADO APRICOT JELLY

1 medium ripe avocado

several slices tinned apricot

1 packet gelatine, any flour

½ pt (¼ litre) hot water

½ pt (¼ litre) cold water

1. Prepare avocado pear. Wash and peel avocado. Cut into thin rings round the seeds. Arrange rings in the serving dish and leave one for decoration. Place apricot slices inside the rings and around the sides. 2. Prepare gelatine. Empty contents of packet into measuring jug. Add hot water and stir until the crystals are dissolved. Add cold water. 3. Pour gelatine immediately over fruits and cool them first in a bowl with cold

water and ice cubes, then put in refrigerator to set. Alternatively, leave jelly till it start setting, then add fruit and leave to set in refrigerator or other cold place.

PRAWN SWEET JELLY (KAMBA)

6 oz (180 g) fresh or frozen prawns

½ packet lemon flavoured gelatine

¾ pt fresh pineapple juice, boiled

1½ tablespoons sugar some tinned cherries for decoration

1. If using fresh prawns, remove the outer hard covering, and cut into pieces.
2. Boil prawns in just enough water for about 10-15 minutes and cool immediately.
3. Squeeze juice from pineapple and boil it. Remove from heat, add gelatine. 4. Stir until all gelatine is dissolved or stand dish with mixture into a pan of boiling water for quick dissolving. 5. Add the sugar into gelatine for more taste, if desired, cool. 6. Fill two moulds with cold water and keep cool in refrigerator or cool place. 7. Mix some of the prawns into other gelatine. 8. Pour water from moulds, put remaining prawns at bottom of each basin. Pour in dissolved gelatine. 9. Leave to set in refrigerator's freezer for about 45 minutes. 10. When set, if possible turn out into a plate decorated with cherries. 11. Serve cold as a sweet.

MILK SWEET

¼ bundle China grass

¼ pt (¼ litre) water

4 oz sugar

1 pt milk

lemon essence or rind

food colouring, if desired

1. Heat water and China grass until it dissolves. 2. Heat milk with lemon rind or essence. 3. Mix dissolved China grass, milk, essence and food colouring, if used. 4. Pour mixture in a wet mould and place in cool place to set. 5. Serve with fresh fruits.

9
RELISHES, PICKLES, RESERVES AND JAMS

VEGETABLE KACHUMBARI

1 large, firm tomato

1 large onion

2 medium carrots

1 small, young cabbage

1 cucumber

1 lemon

1 green chilli

salt to taste

1. Wash and slice tomato and cucumber very thinly. 2. Shred cabbage very finely, and then wash thoroughly in salt water. 3. Wash and grate carrots and a bit of lemon rind. 4. Slice the

chilli. 5. Cut the lemon and squeeze out the juice. 6. Mix all vegetables, add salt and lemon juice. 7. Serve cold with pilau, rice or bananas.

TOMATO CHUTNEY

1 lb (½ kg) tomatoes

1 piece fresh or dried whole ginger

3 cloves garlic

1 onion

1 teaspoon chilli powder

½ teaspoon salt

4 cardamom pods

4 tablespoon sugar

4 tablespoons vinegar

1. Wash and chop tomatoes coarsely. 2. Peel and chop onion and garlic. 3. Crush cardamom seeds and chop ginger. 4. Mix tomatoes, onion, garlic and ginger and cook covered until soft. 5. Add cardamom, vinegar and sugar and continue to cook for another 10-15 minutes, or until the chutney is thick. 6. Pour into a clean, warm jar with a screw top life. 7. Use as required.

CARROT CHUTNEY

1 lb (½ kg) fresh carrots

3 fresh ginger roots

2 whole bulb of garlic (several cloves together)

12 tablespoons sugar

1 teaspoon salt

1 cup vinegar

1 teaspoon chilli powder

2 cardamom pods

½ glass of water

1. Wash, peel and finely shred the carrots. 2. Crush ginger, cardamom pods and garlic. 3. Put sugar in a pan, add water and bring to boil. 4. Add carrots, ginger, cardamom, garlic, salt and chilli and cook for 15-20 minutes. 5. Add vinegar and cook, stirring continuously until quite thick but not dry. 6. Pour into a clean screw top jar while still hot.

PAWPAW ACHARI

4 oz (120 gm) unripe pawpaw

1 teaspoon mustard seeds

1 teaspoon curry powder

½ teaspoon turmeric

1 medium onion, chopped

2 tablespoons lemon juice

1 red chilli with seeds, chopped

2 tablespoons fat or oil

1 level teaspoon salt

1 level teaspoon sugar

1. Prepare pawpaw. Peel unripe pawpaw and cut in lengthwise. Remove seeds, cut pawpaw into even cubes of about 1cm. Wash cubes, and dry thoroughly. 2. Cook pawpaw cubes in water until just tender. Drain. 3. Add onion and chilli, then fry over low heat. 4. Add in the other ingredients and spices, fry until powder and other ingredients are cooked. Add in lemon juice and stir. Serve cold or hot. 5. Suitable for curries and rice.

CARROT SAMBARO

8 oz (240 gm) carrots, grated

1 teaspoon mustard seeds

½ teaspoon turmeric powder

½ teaspoon chilli powder

2 green chilli

½ teaspoon curry powder

3 tablespoons lemon juice or lime juice

3 teaspoons *dengu* flour (lentil flour)

2 tablespoons fat

4 cloves of garlic, chopped

1 level teaspoon sugar

1. Grate carrots, crush garlic, chop green chillies. 2. Heat fat and put in mustard seed, add turmeric powder, chilli powder, curry powder and salt. 3. Fry spices with medium heat. Add carrots, green chillies, cover pot and leave to cook for about 4 minutes. 4. Sprinkle with *dengu* flour, then add some lemon juice. 5. Serve with rice or ugali.

FRIED GREEN PAWPAW (SAMBRO)

½ green pawpaw

1 green chilli

1 tablespoon red palm oil

salt to taste

1 lime

1 onion

1. Wash and peel pawpaw, cut it up into thin short strips. 2. Wash the strips again in plenty of running water to remove the bitter, milky juice. 3. Cook them in boiling water with salt till tender. 4. Skin and chop onion very fine. 5. Strain off cooked

pawpaw. 6. Heat oil in a saucepan and fry onion till golden in colour. 7. Add cooled pawpaws to fat and toss them in the pan. 8. Cut and add green chilli to pawpaws, then add lime juice. 9. When ready, serve hot as an accompaniment for rice, ugali or nay meat dish.

SIKI TOMATO PRESERVE

½ litre lemon juice

4 medium, fresh firm tomatoes

2 onions

Salt

2 green chillies according to taste

1. Clean and sterilize a screw-top jar and lid in boiling water. 2. Wash and cut tomatoes into small pieces. 3. Skin and cut onions into thin rings. 4. Wash and cut chillies in halves and mix them with tomatoes and onion in a bowl. 5. Wash, cut and squeeze out juice of lemon and put in the sterilized jar. 6. Mix all ingredients together and add salt. 7. Pour immediately into jar and screw lid on. 8. Put jar out in sunlight for several days, for 2-3 days or even a week, depending on the intensity of the sun. **NOTE:** Always shake the bottle to mix ingredients. This preserve can be an accompaniment with savoury dishes, e.g. rice. It also adds best to other meals.

ORANGE MARMALADE

2 lb (1 kg) firm oranges

2 lemons

2 pt water

2 lb (1 kg) sugar

1. Wash oranges and lemons. 2. Cut fruits and squeeze out juice, remove seeds. 3. Cut rinds into pieces. 4. Put rinds in a pan. Add water and boil until soft. 5. Remove from water, cool and cut into fine shreds or mince. 6. Return shredded rind into water in the pan, add sugar, fruit juice and stir over low heat until sugar dissolves. 7. Boil

rapidly for 25-30 minutes until marmalade thickens and starts to set. 8. Pour into a warm jar with a screw-top lid while it is hot.

NOTE: To test marmalade is set, drop a little hot marmalade put on a cold plate; it should form a skin immediately.

MAPERA JAM (GUAVA JAM)

20 medium red *mapera*

1½ lb (750 gm) sugar

2 lemons

1. Wash *mapera*, peel and cut fleshy part away from the seeds. 2. Put fleshy parts in one cooking pan and seeds in another. 3. Pour 1 cup water over the fleshy part of fruit and put to boil until tender. 4. Pour ½ cup water over the seedy parts and put to boil. 5. When both are tender, sieve first fleshy parts then seedy parts. 6. Weight the *mapera* if possible, add same amount by weight in sugar. 7. Add juice of two lemons and rind of one lemon. 8. Bring slowly to boil, then boil rapidly for 20 minutes. Check the thickness. 9. Pour hot in clean warm jars and close immediately.

MANGO JAM

2 lb (1 kg) firm ripe mangoes

1 lb (½kg) sugar

3 lemon

1 Wash and peel mangoes. Slice mangoes into thin slices. Discard the stone. 3. Weigh mango slices, measure out on equal amount of sugar. 4. Grate rind from the lemon. Squeeze out juice. 5. Put the mangoes, sugar, lemon rind and juice in a pan. 6. Mix and slowly bring to boil. Raise heat and boil quickly stirring frequently (15-20 minutes) until the jam thickens. 7. Test for setting and skim. 8. Pour into warm screw-top jar while hot. 9. Close the jar and cool.

PINEAPPLE JAM

2 lb (1 kg) pineapple

1½ lb ¾ kg) sugar

2 lemons

1. Peel, then mince or grate pineapple by scraping with a fork or grater. 2. Weigh pineapple pulp and measure out an equal amount of sugar. 3. Grate rind from lemon and squeeze out juice. 4. Put pineapple pulp, sugar, lemon rind and juice in a pan and slowly bring to boil. 5. Increase the heat and quickly boil for 25-30 minutes, or until the jam starts to set, stirring frequently. 6. Skim and pour into a warm screw top jar while it is still hot. 7. Close the jar tightly and leave to cool.

PEACH JAM

2 lb (1 kg) peaches

2 lb (1 kg) sugar

2 lemons

1. Wash peaches and remove stones. 2. Weigh peaches and measure out equal amount of sugar. 3. Slice, then mince or chop peaches. 4. Grate lemon rind and squeeze out juice. 5. Put peach pulp, sugar, lemon rind and juice into a pan and slowly bring to boil until the sugar dissolves. 6. Then boil rapidly for 15-20 minutes until the jam thickens and begins to set. 7. Skim and pour in a warm jar with a screw top while still hot. 8. Close the jar tightly and leave to cool.

INDEX

185

190

196